MAKING THE MOST OF WHAT YOU'VE GOT

Allan D. Willey

HARVEST HOUSE PUBLISHERS
Eugene, Oregon 97402

MAKING THE MOST OF WHAT YOU'VE GOT
Copyright © 1982 Harvest House Publishers
Eugene, Oregon 97402

Library of Congress Catalog Card 82-82410
ISBN 0-89081-393-0

Printed in the United States of America.

Contents

Preface

PREFACE

"God will provide."

Sure he will! But did He provide for the one who hid his talent in the earth (Matt. 25:18)?

"Thou wicked and slothful servant" was the earful that unfortunate heard (Matt. 25:26).

If we all got to write our own greetings from the Lord on Judgment Day, would we not want something like "Well done, good and faithful servant"? Surely that would be the supreme accolade.

How, then, do we take the biblical principles of planting, growing and reaping and apply them to the Lord's benefit in our financial affairs today?

How can we enjoy the abundance, prosperity and riches referred to so often in the Bible, use them to increase our own wealth, and in turn be more able to provide for others?

How do we multiply our resources and practice good Christian stewardship in today's confusing world of conflicting demands?

Is it possible to tithe with ease—and then give more?

This book will answer all those questions and more. It will show how to manage your money properly today, how to apply your spiritual learning in times of inflation and high income taxes.

"Seek ye first the kingdom of God, and his righteousness; and all these things shall be added unto you" (Matt. 6:33). Note the sequence: first the Kingdom of God. Without that primary commitment to God and His work, you cannot expect God's blessing on any financial plan. The wicked may prosper for a time on this earth, but such bounty is only temporary at best, and no life can be fully satisfying apart from God. But if you begin with a wholehearted devotion to God and want to be a good steward of the financial resources He entrusts to you, this book will help you understand how to "provide... for those of his own house" (1 Tim. 5:8).

There are financial and investment opportunities now as never before, and it is our Christian duty to learn about and take advantage of them. This book is going to sow the seeds of knowledge for proper personal money management and prosperity.

The principles outlined apply to the vast majority of the population and should be used by them without change. Inevitably, there will be some readers who have specialized knowledge and skills in some of the areas covered, and in those instances they should bend the rules to take advantage of the skill they have. For example, artisans in the building trade may buy different single family rental homes from those specified, as they can profit from their technical knowledge. Likewise, a stockbroker or corporate executive may be comfortable investing a higher proportion of his assets in the stock market than is advocated, and he should also take advantage of his knowledge. However, most people are unaware of the basic principles of personal money management, and that is causing unnecessary hardship.

This book is for those who already own their personal residence (or have given it serious thought) and desire to increase their net worth. It is written for those who have their spiritual lives in order (in the sense of having surrendered every area of their lives to Christ's lordship) and need to understand today's conditions to put their financial lives in order.

It is for those who are not afraid of work and risk, for those who trust that God put them on earth for a purpose, part of which being that by their prosperity they can help others.

CHAPTER 1

In the Money Game

Money Is Not a Static Subject

"Jesus Christ the same yesterday, and today, and for ever" (Heb. 13:8). Religious beliefs and principles are fixed, openly discussed, and relatively easy to study and learn from the "manufacturer's handbook."

Contrast that topic with money management, which is not a fixed subject. It is continually changing. When the media are flooded with stories about gold and silver, the public buys gold and silver. When real estate is focused on, people wheel and deal in property. If money market funds are featured, everyone goes out and invests in a money market fund.

The problem is that that is piecemeal investing. The new information is being added to old information, which may well be erroneous to begin with or out-of-date. And there is no one fount of accurate financial information. Instead, there are almost as many views as there are economists and financial counselors.

Source of Information

How did we learn about personal money management? It is not taught in schools. Most of us learned from our parents. Our parents taught us to be thrifty, to save, and to put our money in the bank, there it tended to earn interest and grow. If there were excess funds in the bank, we tended to put those on the stock market, and that tended to grow, too. But we have never taken the trouble to relearn the rules. That may have been good advice in the days when we were being brought up, but it is certainly not the way to manage your money properly today.

Times have changed. Our parents' money learning took place in days when there was minimal inflation. The same rules are not applicable when inflation is a major factor.

We have also adopted bad habits because we were raised in the land of plenty. Sure, we may be good Christians, hard-working and reasonably thrifty, but we still have developed wasteful habits and careless spending patterns. Our appreciation of money and knowledge of its power are infinitesimal compared to that of those who have little. People in underprivileged countries have very few coins flowing through their fingers in the course of a year. They tend to know the value of each coin and what it will bring.

CHANGE

Individuals are subject to continual change, both of a personal nature and in the world around them. This change is happening much more rapidly than people are aware of, and it has a drastic effect on their personal money management.

Changes of a personal nature are such things as:
We get out of school.
We start a career.
We get married.
We raise a family.
We get a promotion or a new career.
A spouse goes to work.
A child goes to college.
We reach middle age.
A child leaves home.
We retire.

At all these stages of our personal development, our monetary requirements are totally different. You are obviously going to make a different financial decision going into retirement from the one you would make when you first start out on your career.

Then, coupled with those personal changes, there is a whole series of external influences—most of them out of our control. One external influence we can control is further education, which is essential for our personal money management progress. But influences we cannot control include

> health
> inheritance
> financial setback
> civil unrest
> war
> business cycles
> natural disasters
> technological advance
> legislation
> and a whole host of others.

Most of us have bought a calculator in recent years because of the tremendous technological advances in that product. That is an example of change affecting our financial or investment decisions.

In August 1981, President Reagan signed into law a tax package known as ERTA, the Economic Recovery Tax Act of 1981. By a stroke of the pen, he totally altered everyone's financial and investment options. The provisions of that act alone have precipitated buy or sell decisions for virtually every taxpayer.

We will examine how to monitor and record those changes so that we can take advantage of them in our financial decisions.

NO GOOD SOURCE OF UP-TO-DATE INFORMATION

Strange as it may seem, there is no good source of money management information today. There appears to be, but that in itself is a problem. The government wants every citizen to pay taxes. The financial institutions plead for us to deposit our money with them. Books are written on the stock market, real estate, and commodities. There are "get rich quick" seminars. The Wall Street Journal is published 5 days a week, and newspapers have their business sections. There appears to be a mass of information available to the public.

But the "public" is different. It is you and I. We are individuals. We are unique. True, we are all one under God, but our monetary needs, wants, and desires are totally different.

One of the basic problems of the published money management information is that the writers do not identify who the information applies to. Let me avoid that error by saying that this book is written for all taxpayers with annual family earnings under $100,000 and a net worth under $1 million. Those are maximum numbers, because in fact it will be read by those who are at the lower end of that scale and want to know how to reach the upper end. The path to financial prosperity for individuals in that category will be defined in this book.

Contrast that definition of readership with that of The Wall Street Journal, which is the organ of big business. It is written for the executives of the Fortune 500 companies—both the first and the second 500. Many of those people earn more than $100,000 per year, and their net worth is often higher than $1 million. Therefore, their principles of net worth accumulation are totally different. This is in no way a criticism of that excellent newspaper, but it is vital that readers understand who The Wall Street Journal is written for so that they can properly form their conclusions from the information given. The Journal should not be read by the average taxpayer for financial advice, but it is valuable reading for a good steward who needs to keep up-to-date with economic trends and topical items of interest.

GOVERNMENT AND FINANCIAL INSTITUTIONS

The government and financial institutions give us misinformation. Sure, everyone has to pay taxes—that is, everyone who has not taken the trouble to find out how not to reduce their income tax payment. With the rules that are on the books today, there is no reason a careful Christian can not reduce their payment of taxes.

The government publicizes heavily the unemployment figure: "We have 8 percent unemployment"; "10 percent of the people are out of work"; and so on. The reason that number is so important to the government is that its income is based on employment. The larger the workforce, the more it receives in taxes, Social Security contributions, and on down the line. The smaller the workforce, the fewer funds it has available to spend on political programs such as defense, and the more it must pay out in public assistance.

A movement of 1 percent in the unemployment rate is of major consequence to the government, and its spokesmen scream and holler and fill the media with dire predictions when the unemployment rate exceeds its expectations.

But to you and me, 8 percent unemployment means that 92 percent are employed. That is outstanding! Ninety-one percent is a figure to rejoice in! And so is 90 percent. Misleading, biased information is published by the government because it materially affects it, but it is confusing to the ordinary taxpayer who is striving to achieve good Christian stewardship.

The same is true of the financial institutions. They want depositors' money so that they can earn a profit by lending out the funds in the economy. A good Christian steward will recognize the problems caused by this passive form of investing and invest directly in the economy with superior returns.

THE PEOPLE SOURCE

If there is no good source of published information on personal money management, how about a people source? Who can a taxpayer go to for advice and information on financial matters? A list of sources would include

> parents
> relatives
> friends
> C.P.A.
> attorney
> banker
> stock broker
> real estate broker
> insurance agent
> financial consultant

There are problems with each of those people, too, except, maybe the last one.

We have already discussed the problem with using financial information from parents—it is probably out-of-date. Advice from other relatives and friends tends to be specialized and does not take into account that individuals are unique. Uncle Joe or Aunt Susie may be happy, successful, and prosperous, but just because they used their individual talents to advantage does not mean their policies can be adopted profitably by another.

Certified Public Accountants deal with history. They look backward. They file tax returns and conduct audits. That is historical information. Financial advice should be obtained from someone who only looks forward, who considers the financial condition of the family, regardless of how they got there, and points them in the right direction.

An attorney's function concerns the law, and a banker specializes in borrowing and lending money. Neither is equipped to give good advice on increasing net worth.

Stockbrokers, real estate agents, and insurance agents deal with specific money products and should not be relied on to give unbiased advice in areas other than their own products.

There is, therefore, a vacuum in the area of good financial advice and advisers to give it, yet the public needs the information. Most people cannot understand how tens of thousands of dollars of earnings (way beyond their wildest dreams when they started their careers) can be flowing through their fingers and yet they do not have the cash to buy groceries. They do not understand how they can be worth twenty, forty, or eighty thousand dollars and more—probably tied up in the equity in their homes— and yet they cannot afford to pay their bills.

FINANCIAL COUNSELING

Because of the above, financial counseling is a profession of the future. People need someone they can sit down with, someone to whom they can explain their financial situation, and who will give them answers to their questions and show them the path to financial security and the counters to inflation and income taxes.

The financial counselor will provide a checkup similar to a medical checkup. In the old days, if we had a pain, we went to the general practitioner, the family doctor. He made a diagnosis and then if necessary, sent us on to whatever specialist we needed—heart, ears, nose and throat, etc.

Financial consultants should operate in the same way. Their pay should be a *fee*, not a commission. They identify the problem, make recommendations to cure the problem and then send the family to one of the specialists for implementation.

However, there is a problem when we seek professional help nowadays. We're scared to talk! We know that as soon as we open our mouths, the time clock starts ticking. A few weeks after our visit, we get a bill in our mailbox and exclaim, "Did I talk that much?"

The need, therefore, is for a financial consultant who will charge a *fixed fee* for whatever it takes—time, meetings, correspondence, phone calls—until everyone around that table agrees, "Yes, this is what we should be doing." No agreement, no fee!

The job of the consultant is not to find the investments, but to give the *best* advice for that particular family's circumstances and then direct them to one of the specialists mentioned. For example, suppose you have an estate tax problem. The consultant would tell you to see an estate tax attorney and discuss trusts. Or perhaps you are overpaying income taxes. The solution is to get some more income tax deductions. The consultant might suggest you buy some improved real estate through a real estate broker.

The consultant would then explain those solutions in more specific detail so the family is better equipped to hire the proper professional help and implement the solution.

COMMISSION-BASED FINANCIAL PLANNERS

If you look in the Yellow Pages, you will probably find some people listed who call themselves financial planners. They are often members of the International Association of Financial Planners, which is their trade association. Many of these financial planners have the designation C.F.P., or Certified Financial Planner.

However, we see a problem with seeking financial advice from this particular kind of counselor. If you go into their offices, it is like walking into a financial supermarket. They will sell you a product off the shelf under the guise of financial planning—something like an oil and gas tax shelter, real estate syndication, diamonds, or mutual funds. That is not the financial counseling the public needs and wants, in our opinion. How can you be an unbiased financial adviser if you are going to make a commission from your recommendations?

Worse still, many (not all, obviously), of those C.F.P's take great delight in delving into the smallest financial detail, churning out reams of statistics on the computer and then charging the customer sometimes as much as $4,000 for a "financial plan." They then act as the true salespeople they are and sell the client products to implement the plan.

A good financial consultant, on the other hand, can do a better job for clients by identifying the one or two items with greatest priority and largest financial impact, charge a fixed fee of up to say $500, and then repeat the process as required (on an annual basis at least).

Many of these consultants belong to the Society of Financial Consultants and carry the designation S.F.C.

PROFESSIONAL ADVISERS

At the end of this section is a list of professional advisers a person would need on a continuing basis during his lifetime for financial advice and assistance. The advisers are listed in the approximate order that their services will be required by a person starting out on careful personal money management. Those professionals are normally found by referral, but even after the best references have been obtained, it is still a matter of personal chemistry between the professional and the client. All too frequently, a client will stay on with a professional adviser after the client has lost confidence in him.

The best place to go for referrals is to someone with a similar background and circumstances. For example, a young couple seeking to buy a house would check with their young friends who were already homeowners about a good real estate agent. A couple seeking advice regarding inheritance taxes would likewise ask about an estate tax attorney among their friends who had sizable estates.

Since the client-professional union should be long term, it would be unusual to have a major age difference between the two. An elderly lady would work better with an older attorney in drawing up a will. A young, forward-looking couple would bank where there was a young, aggressive bank manager.

These are the professionals you're likely to need throughout your lifetime, in the order in which you're most apt to need them:

> banker
> accountant
> insurance agent
> attorney
> financial consultant
> real estate broker
> stockbroker

Keep in mind that although each of those has a particular role to play in your personal money management, the financial consultant, when you're ready for him, ought to be your primary source of information and advice.

WE ARE ALL IN THE MONEY GAME

In days gone by, an individual could follow his chosen profession, practice thrift, and at the completion of his working life retire and live comfortably from the proceeds of that thrift. That is not true any more. Thrift will no longer insure a comfortable retirement. In fact, putting money in the bank is a passive investment and will *lose* money for the depositor.

You have to be an active investor today if you ever want to reach financial security. The days of succeeding as a passive investor ceased when inflation came in to stay. In other words, each day you either gain ground or lose it in your battle against inflation and for financial security.

We all live and work in a capitalistic society. We like the benefits of capitalism, so we participate in capitalism. Give and ye shall receive. Capitalism is based on intelligent people working hard to make a living and risking their funds to make even more money.

You cannot decide for yourself if you want to play the money game. You are in it. You are on the team. You should learn the rules now so you can play it properly—and win.

RETIREMENT

If you retire at age sixty or sixty-five, you can anticipate living for another twenty or twenty-five years. That is a long period of time to support yourself and a spouse without employment earnings, so you need other sources of income. They can include

> Social Security
> pension plan
> personal investments

Let's look briefly at each of those sources.

Social Security. Social Security was not designed to be the sole source of retirement income when it was originally put into effect. For many, however, it has assumed that mantle. The Social Security Fund is on a road to bankruptcy, as there are fewer and fewer workers contributing to it, whereas the number of recipients increases as people live longer. The government will have to tinker with the system, curtailing benefits and increasing the age at which they become payable, in order to keep the program solvent.

Thus, it would be unwise for anyone to count on a Social Security check as a major portion of their retirement earnings, and anyone not retiring in the very near future should certainly anticipate that their benefits will only become payable at a later age than is now the case.

The Social Security rules also brainwash people into believing what their working life span should be. The sixty-two or sixty-five age at which benefits become payable represents a "goal line" to be reached by the worker. The implication is also that when this "retirement" starts, the individual can enjoy the rest and relaxation he has "earned" during his working life.

No good Christian steward will be fooled by this way of thinking, as it is a certain path to hardship. A Christian serves God first and does not ever quit that service. A good Christian steward also realizes that working for someone else is only one of the many ways to produce income, and that working to produce income from investments is not tied to any age limit.

Pension Plan. Many organizations have heavily mortgaged their future earnings by providing too liberal pension benefits for employees. It may be justifiable to award pension rights to an individual after twenty years of service, but surely this should only start being paid out on leaving the workforce at a normal retirement age. People drawing pensions from one employer while yet in their forties, and at the same time participating in the work force in another job, place an undue burden on the employer, co-workers, and the country.

The city of San Francisco, for example, had extraordinarily costly police and firemen's pension benefits approved by voters in 1974. Generous cost-of-living increases created an extremely high potential cost for the city. Mayor Feinstein's administration recognized the problem, and the voters in 1980 approved a program whereby the city would offer to buy out each individual's ultra-expensive pension rights for immediate cash payments of up to $40,000. It is not too surprising that only a few accepted the offer.

Because of those liberal pension benefits already granted, plus inflation and a declining workforce to pay into pension plans in the future, a retiree cannot count on receiving an adequate pension from a union or employer's benefit plan.

The government has recognized the seriousness of the problem its citizens are heading into, and we have recently received its encouragement to set up our own pension funds. Individual Retirement Accounts and Keogh plans are a vital ingredient of personal money management and will be discussed in detail later.

Personal Investments. The foregoing comments on Social Security and pension plans underline the importance of developing and maintaining a sound investment program during one's normal working life. It will be the proper planting, growing, and harvesting of selected investments that will determine the comfort level of an individual's retirement years.

To avoid the disappointment that will be ours in later years if we neglect to take advantage of present financial opportunities, let us look at some important principles in personal money management.

CHAPTER 2

Principles of
Personal Money Management

SPEND TIME ON PERSONAL MONEY MANAGEMENT

The first principle, often overlooked, is that *you have to spend time on personal money management.* "Now, wait a minute," you say. "I already have demands on my time that exceed the hours in the day—church, church functions, Bible study, and family, to name a few. The politicians tell me I am apathetic about politics and demand I pay more attention to current affairs. The teachers insist I join a committee and assist in the children's education. The community complains because I am not active in local affairs. I cannot find time to fix the washing machine, clean the car, or rake the yard, and now I have to spend time on personal money management!"

That's right!

Ten to twenty percent of the time you spend earning your money has got to be spent on managing it—and this applies to all the family earners. It may require a readjustment of priorities to find the time, but the rewards are great. *If you spend that time on personal money management, you will make as much if not more from managing your money as you ever do from earning it in the first place, regardless of how little or how much you start off with.* That is the first principle of stewardship—spend time on it.

The paying of bills (your record-keeping system may need

streamlining), continually reading and learning about the subject, and selecting and maintaining investments can all be pleasurable and useful *if* the family has formed a sound financial strategy.

EVERY TAXPAYER IS IN BUSINESS

The next principle in personal money management is that, as a good Christian steward, *you must recognize that you are in business.* The word *business* is used just as it is used for any other business in the country.

We are in business the same as Sears, I.B.M., General Motors, the local church, the "mom and pop" grocery store, or a laundromat. In fact, every taxpayer is in at least two businesses. They are the earning power business and the net worth business. Until now we have been using the term "personal money management," but from now on we will refer to net worth.

Determine your: Assets
take away your: (Liabilities),
and that gives you your: *Net Worth.*

or

what you Own
less what you (Owe)
equals your *Net Worth.*

We may, of course, be in many more than two businesses. For example, an author may have several earning businesses such as

financial seminars
financial consulting
writing books

A family may have separate net worth businesses.

savings
real estate investments
stock market investments

Those businesses are separately funded and must be separately managed according to the principles that apply to any other business.

FIVE BUSINESS COMPONENTS

Let us examine what a business is and how it operates. Any business, regardless of size, can be broken down into five major components.

These are
> purchasing
> production
> administration
> marketing
> selling

Take, for example, a clothing manufacturer. We all acknowledge that a clothing manufacturer is in business, so what is meant by the *purchasing* function of that business? We can visualize that the clothing manufacturer has employees who go out and buy cloth, thread, buttons and other items from suppliers. That is the purchasing function.

What is the *production* function? Again, we can picture that the clothing manufacturer has an industrial building full of machinery and employees that cut, stitch and sew the finished product, a suit of clothes. That is the production function.

What is included in *administration*? Administration is the entire realm of paperwork in that business. The payroll, accounts receivable, inventory records, legal and tax matters, financial statements—all are included in the administration of the business.

What is *marketing*? It is the portrayal of that business to the trade and the public at large. Marketing is the public relations, the packaging, the advertising. Marketing is the *attracting* of customers.

Note that marketing is totally different from *selling*, because selling is only the conversion of the inventory into cash. It is the culmination of all the other functions.

Now, if you are to be successful in business, you have to be operating adequately in all five of these business components. If you are weak or shaky in any one of them, you are heading for serious trouble.

Consider again the clothing manufacturer. Let us say the purchasing department does a first-rate job. The buyers buy the finest cloth and supplies that are available. Production also works admirably. There is never a button that falls off, a seam that splits or a thread that is loose. Marketing such high-quality garments is relatively straightforward, and when those garments reach the retail stores, they sell quickly from the racks. And the clothing manufacturer goes under! The company fails.

Why?

Sure, they were buying very high quality cloth and making very fine garments, but they were a few weeks behind in their paperwork. Their administrative function was a little shaky. What administration was not telling management was that it was expensive to buy that fine cloth. And maybe to produce such high-quality garments there were extra employees on the production line. What was costing $500 a suit to produce, they were selling for $300. If they keep that up for just a short time, they will go under.

Is it not true that if we keep any information at all in either of our two businesses, it is to complete our income tax returns on April 15 each year? So the second important principle of personal money management is that we have to run it like a business and use the techniques that other businesses use. Those include

goals
budgeting
profit projection
quarterly and annual financial statements.

EARNING BUSINESS

Let us see how those five business functions apply to an individual's earning business, because if your earning business is not stable, you cannot make the proper moves to increase your net worth. You cannot be down on your job or your employer and expect to have the right mental attitude for investing. The Bible says it this way, "Servants, obey in all things your masters according to the flesh; not with eye-service, as menpleasers; but in singleness of heart, fearing God" (Col. 3:22).

In our earning business, the purchasing function is the education and training we have taken to obtain skills that can be used to produce wages. That is a never-ending process, as the changes discussed earlier are ever present. Many people do not keep up their education and training aggressively enough, since they feel secure in their jobs. Then in later years they wonder why they have been replaced by someone who has taken the time and effort to keep up-to-date. School is never out for those who want to succeed.

Unfortunately, too many people feel that society owes them a living—again, part of the misinformation provided by the government and media. This attitude can be found among both recent college graduates and long-time employees. The attitude of the recent graduate seems to be: "Hi, society! I spent all these years and dollars getting this fine degree. Now please deliver my 9-to-5, five-days-a-week job—with pension, medical and vacation plans and other fringe benefits, $25,000 per year, minimum supervision, and in an activity that fulfills my great intelligence."

Or the displaced employee says: "I worked in that factory for thirty years, faithfully putting those slide rules together, and all of a sudden they close the plant. I'm a good worker, honest, conscientious, reliable, don't call in sick..."

Sorry, college graduate. Sorry, slide rule connector. It doesn't work that way.

The college degree is the license to start learning how to work your way to success. You now have to find a job opening and take it. Then, by using all your skills, initiative, ingenuity, people relations and continued learning, you may progress through the work force. It is up to you only and your initiative and hard work at any level of employment. No one *owes* you anything.

Sorry, long-time employee. Sure you were a good worker, but your employer did not close the plant "all of a sudden." For years the product has been on the wane and you were just as aware of that as your employer was. Instead of going home at night to watch television, then spending all weekend fishing, maybe you should have been getting some further education at night school.

In later years, if your employer's pay scales have not kept pace with your knowledge and experience, you may have to consider going through the marketing function again to sell yourself to a new employer with better privileges. Again, it is important to distinguish between *your* rights and an employer's obligations. In the capitalist economy, you have the freedom to determine where you want to work, and it should be your continuing goal to maximize your potential and market your skills to the highest bidder. That is a perfectly legitimate (though obviously not the only) factor to consider in determining God's will for your vocational life.

Production as regards our earning power is the meshing together of the learned skills to make it into a marketable product. A math major may combine that knowledge with computer technology to obtain a job in the electronics field. A nurse may take time management & leadership training to tie to the nursing training and equip themself for a supervisory position.

Administration in the earning business is not arduous. Remember, however, that administration includes statistics as well as dollar and cents record keeping so it may be advisable to keep a note of what the demand is for similar skills in other areas and the pay scales. The other side of administration would include the depositing of the paycheck through preparation of the tax return and maintaining knowledge and details of any benefit programs from the government and the employer. Many people are blissfully unaware of their rights in these areas.

Marketing our earning skills is easily understood but goes further than just making ourselves available in the employment market. We must market our skills so that the best job is secured at the best possible price. In later years if our employer's pay scales have not kept pace with our knowledge and experience, we have to go through the marketing function again and sell ourselves to a new employer with better privileges.

Selling as with the clothing manufacturer is the conversion of the inventory into cash. Once we have selected the employer, it is the selling of ourself so that we are hired and not someone else and thus our endeavors are translated into a paycheck.

In going through these five functions as they relate to our earning business you will already have identified areas where you or some of your friends are weak or have not kept up and of course, they are heading for trouble just like the clothing manufacturer.

It is vital in our personal money management that we recognize that we are in business. We must continually develop and upgrade the talents God has given us so that we can be sure that we can turn five into ten or two into four.

CHAPTER 3

Preparation of
Net Worth Statement

Know What You Are Worth

Many people have no idea what their net worth is. How can you expect to manage your money properly if you do not know how much you have to start with? Do you think that any other business or corporation does not know every minute of every day exactly what its assets and liabilities are?

Why do we work today? Why do we take the trouble to produce a paycheck? Certainly it is to put bread and butter on the table, to feed, shelter, and clothe the family. But is it not also to increase our net worth? Let us say your net worth were suddenly two, three, or five million dollars. Would you be doing then what you are doing today? It is doubtful. A major reason we are going to work is to increase our net worth. Let us get it out in the open and start measuring it on a regular basis.

You can find a form at a bank with preprinted headings and as often as not some accounting mumbo jumbo, but it is best to list your net worth on a multi-columned form. If the assets and liabilities are listed in the left-hand column, it is easy in the future to write in the current values in a new column.

ESTIMATE TODAY'S VALUES

We are looking for a list of what we own, less what we owe. Conservative, round number, ballpark estimates of today's values of each item will do. We are going to list only the items we can use to make money with, not those items that are essential to daily living. For example, a refrigerator, washing machine, and furniture are all assets, but they are an integral part of our daily existence. A house, however, though certainly part of our daily needs, is more of an investment and would be listed.

What follows is a simple form for calculating net worth, listing the most common assets and liabilities on such a statement. Liabilities are italicized.

	Round Amount
Personal residence	$
Mortgages thereon	
Other real estate (list)	
Mortgages thereon	
Insurance cash value	
Pension, Keogh, or IRA accounts	
Savings and where held (list)	
Stocks (list)	
Autos	
Loans thereon	
Any other assets (list)	
Any other liabilities (list)	
Paying hobbies	_____
Total assets	
Total liabilities	_____
Subtract for net worth	_____

A paying hobby is something done in our leisure time that can be turned into cash. Many people have collected items over the years—antiques, stamps, coins, baseball cards, and many other items—that technically should be called investments. The question, then, is when does it cease to be a hobby and become material enough to be considered in the investment category? An arbitrary 10 percent of the value of the total assets is recommended. If the value is under 10 percent consider it a hobby; if it's over 10 percent, estimate the value and include it on the net worth statement.

LEVERAGE RATIO

The next step is to calculate your leverage ratio. To do that, divide your total liabilities by the total assets, and express the answer as a percentage. For example:

Total assets		$100,000
Total liabilities		(30,000)
Net worth		70,000
Leverage	30,000 ÷ 100,000 =	30%

In other words, 30 percent of the total value of the assets is owed.

What is the significance of that figure?

We know that financial institutions are willing to lend up to 80 percent of the value of a house. If a couple made a down payment of $20,000 on a house worth $100,000, that would be 80 percent leveraged. Eighty percent is then regarded as the top end of the leverage scale, the bottom being zero.

What should a person's leverage ratio be? In inflationary times, it may be prudent to borrow money to make money. For a young couple just starting out in life, it may not be unusual for them to be 80 percent leveraged. They may be at the top end of the leverage scale. As you go through life from youth to old age, so you may go down the leverage scale, from 80 percent down to zero.

The leverage ratio is one of the items used to measure whether a family is on the right track with its personal money management, and examples of this measurement will be studied later.

EARNINGS

The next number to identify is the annual gross earnings of the family from whatever source. Gross income is income before any payroll deductions and has nothing to do with the check deposited in the bank. There are a lot of people who do not even know what their annual gross earnings are.

For those in business, the earnings figure sought would be the equivalent figure to a paycheck—in other words, the profit of the business after all expenses have been paid.

Gross earnings is the same as the number on the front page of the personal income tax return.

INCOME TAXES PAID

The income taxes paid for the previous year are taken from the personal income tax return. There is a separate line on the tax return that identifies the final calculated tax bill for the year, regardless of how it is paid.

"We didn't pay any income taxes—we got a refund!" many people say.

"We got a bigger refund than ever this year!" some would even say.

Those remarks clearly identify the lack of knowledge of personal money management that people have. Just because you get a refund does not mean to say you did not pay taxes. What it does say is that you committed the cardinal sin of personal money management by giving the government an interest-free loan of your money. How to avoid that situation will be discussed later.

What we need to know now is the total income taxes paid for the year, federal plus state and local taxes, if applicable.

For most people, income taxes paid are the single largest annual expenditure in the entire earning business. They are bigger than food, bigger than clothing, bigger than any form of house payment—rent or mortgage. Taxes are the single largest expense item, and they run totally out of control. But they are paid only by those people who have not applied themselves to their personal money management and have not taken advantage of the many perfectly legal ways to avoid paying them. Just because you do not see them, touch them, or feel them—just because they slide right out of the paycheck—does not mean that income taxes are not real.

Taxes are money!

Taxes are controllable!

In fact, reduction of taxes is the key to proper personal money management. At the moment, we just need to identify how much they total. Later we will find out how to control them.

INCOME TAX RATES

The Economic Recovery Tax Act of 1981, ERTA, "Reagan's tax package," or whatever name you give it, included major tinkering with the income tax rates. The following are examples of tax tables for a married person in the state of California for the federal rates for 1983 and 1984. You can find similar tables for your married status and domicile as required.

Married Taxpayers Filing Jointly and Surviving Spouses				
Taxable Income	1983 % on Pay + Excess		1984 % on Pay + Excess	
$ - 3,400	$ 0	0	$ 0	0
3,400- 5,500	0	11	0	11
5,500- 7,600	231	13	231	12
7,600- 11,900	504	15	483	14
11,900- 16,000	1,149	17	1,085	16
16,000- 20,200	1,846	19	1,741	18
20,200- 24,600	2,644	23	2,497	22
24,600- 29,900	3,656	26	3,465	25
29,900- 35,200	5,034	30	4,790	28
35,200- 45,800	6,624	35	6,274	33
45,800- 60,000	10,344	40	9,772	38
60,000- 85,600	16,014	44	15,168	42
85,600-109,400	27,278	48	25,920	45
109,400-162,400	38,702	50	36,630	49
162,400-215,400	65,202	50	62,600	50
215,400-	91,702	50	89,100	50

State of California Income Tax Table
(for reference only)

Taxable Income		1982 Pay + % on Excess
$ 0 - $ 5,850		1%
5,850 - 10,050	$ 59 +	2% of amount over 5,850
10,050 - 14,250	143 +	3% of amount over 10,050
14,250 - 18,650	269 +	4% of amount over 14,250
18,650 - 22,950	445 +	5% of amount over 18,650
22,950 - 27,150	660 +	6% of amount over 22,950
27,150 - 31,550	912 +	7% of amount over 27,150
31,550 - 35,750	1,220 +	8% of amount over 31,550
35,750 - 40,050	1,556 +	9% of amount over 35,750
40,050 - 44,350	1,943 +	10% of amount over 40,050
44,350 - & over	2,373 +	11% of amount over 44,350

We have reproduced the tables showing percentages. It is interesting to note that many published tables nowadays omit the percentages and just have you read off a tax figure opposite a certain income level. That is a shrewd public relations move on the part of the governing body, as it keeps the taxed public unaware of how high the rates are. If the public was aware that 20, 30 or 40 percent of its income was being paid out in taxes, it might be motivated to take remedial action.

The tax rates that we need to know are the paid rate and the effective tax rate (also frequently referred to as the income tax bracket).

INCOME TAX PAID RATE

The paid rate is the easy one to understand. Divide the total annual taxes paid by the total earnings, and give the answer as a percentage. For example:

$$\frac{\text{Total annual taxes}}{\text{Total annual earnings}} = \frac{6,000}{30,000} = 20\% = \text{paid rate}$$

In other words, of every income dollar earned, 20 percent was paid out in income taxes.

Is 20 percent high?

It most certainly is, and your income tax paid rate is probably higher. Compare your tax paid rate, for example, with what a bank pays in interest. Remember, too, that this income tax rate is the average rate paid on *every* income dollar. Fortunately, income taxes are controllable, unlike other taxes or levies such as sales tax, Social Security, union dues, and unemployment or disability deductions.

One sign of good Christian stewardship is to pay more in tithes and charitable contributions than one pays in income taxes. That is a goal worth pursuing.

GRADUATED INCOME TAX TABLE

We need to know next what would be paid in taxes if we earned *more* money. It is important to recognize that the tables are graduated. A person with $24,000 in earnings will pay much more than double the taxes of someone earning $12,000.

Let's take an example. From the table we read that a taxable income of about $12,000 will result in a federal tax bill of just over $1,085. Roughly 9 percent of the income will be paid in taxes in other words. Sounds like tithing! Logically, it would then seem that for those who took the trouble to double their earnings, they should pay twice as much in taxes. Going further, if they really tried to advance their careers by detailed study and personal advancement and so earned three or five times as much, their tax bill should logically be three or five times as great. Let's compare that in tabular form with what actually happens.

Taxable Income	Taxes should be	Taxes are
$12,000	1,085	
x2 = 24,000	x2 = 2,170	$ 3,465
x3 = 36,000	x2 = 3,255	$ 6,274
x5 = 60,000	x2 = 3,255	$15,168

At the $60,000 level, instead of 9 percent being paid out in taxes, the figure has rocketed all the way to almost 25 percent!

INCOME TAX BRACKET

The question is now "What would the tax consequences be if we made more than our current earnings?"

The increased earnings can be from any source—pay raise,

bonus, increased commission, better rate of interest on savings, increasing the rents on rental property, and so on.

If the earnings had to increase from, for example, $29,900 to $30,900, a $1,000 increase, what would the tax rate be on the extra $1,000? The table tells us that in the third column—28 percent. In other words, on that last $1,000 of earnings, $280 would be paid in federal taxes.

To this must be added the state and local tax rates to arrive at the effective tax rate, or tax bracket. Continuing the $1,000 example through to the California tax tables, we read 7 percent. So in California, a couple with taxable income of $30,900 would be in the 35 percent (28 percent + 7 percent) income tax bracket.

What is true for more income is also true for more income tax deductions. If the couple reduced their taxable income from $29,900 to $28,900 by seeking out an additional $1,000 of deductions, they would reduce their taxes by $350, which is 35 percent of $1,000.

The income tax bracket is a very important number. *It is the number that governs investment decisions.* Are we out there looking for investments that *add* to our taxable income, knowing that 35 percent of any increase will be paid over in taxes? Or are we out there looking for investments that will result in income tax deductions knowing that 35 percent of each additional dollar of deductions found will reduce the tax bill by thirty-five cents?

We now have all the information available to work on our personal money management. However, *all* that information must be examined. Even just one item missing can result in wrong decisions being made, so we have to know

      individual assets
      individual liabilities
      net worth
      leverage percentage
      annual gross earnings
      total income taxes paid
      income tax paid rate
      income tax bracket

A completed net worth statement of a couple may appear as follows:

Personal residence		$100,000
Mortgage thereon		(39,000)
Rental house		60,000
Mortgage		(20,000)
Insurance cash value		2,000
I.R.A.		---
Savings—bank		3,000
Stocks		---
Autos		5,000
Auto loan		(1,000)
Total assets		$170,000
Total liabilities		(60,000)
Net worth		$110,000
Leverage		35%
Gross earnings		$ 35,000
28% Income taxes—federal	$5,000	
7% state	1,000	
Total taxes	$6,000	
Paid rate		17%
35% Effective rate		

Based on these rough and estimated figures, we can begin to count the cost and determine action.

Let us now analyze the net worth statement to determine what action needs to be taken.

CHAPTER 4

Analysis of Net Worth Statement

EXAMINE QUARTERLY

"Be thou diligent to know the state of thy flock, and look well to thy herds" (Prov. 27:23). Not too many people own flocks and herds these days, and the increased specialization and diversification of employment have made money the common medium of exchange.

The instruction from the Bible is, however, still true and commonly overlooked. We are going to identify the problem areas in the net worth statement so that the proper remedial action can be taken.

First of all, the analysis of the net worth statement should be done quarterly. With practice, it can be done in only a few minutes. Not every item will vary each quarter, but with circumstances changing as rapidly as they do, there is a need to examine progress on a regular, systematic basis. There is also a relationship between each item on the net worth statement. Whenever assets are bought or sold, the relationship changes, and that in itself may necessitate other moves having to be made.

For example, the sale of stock would increase the cash on hand and may also increase the taxable income. The surplus cash may then have to be reinvested in an asset, such as real estate, which may yield deductions to reduce the taxable income.

The inability of people to understand that all the items in the net worth statement are interwoven and have a relationship to each other is one of the fatal flaws in personal money management.

ANALYSIS OF NET WORTH STATEMENT

There are many reasons for a person to make financial decisions that change the net worth statement. The following is a list of twenty-two of the most common of those situations, and it should be emphasized that a change *has* to be made if *any* of the following items is true.

1. *Personal residence needs to be changed.* The existing residence is not the most suitable place for the family to be living in for the next three years. The residence should be the right size, shape, and location for the needs, wants, and desires of the family, with prudent limitations.

2. *Equity in personal residence is too high.* There is too much equity in the personal residence, and taxes paid are high.

3. *The personal residence has more than one mortgage against it.* Generally speaking, there is financial security in having only a first mortgage against the personal residence. The reason is that if there is ever a cash shortage, you can always get a second loan using the house as security.

4. *The personal residence has a loan against it that has a short-term balloon payment due, and you probably won't be able to pay it.* Since the personal residence is the best investment a family owns, it should have secure, long-term financing against it.

5. *A rental property has excess equity, and taxes paid are high.* The equity can be used to purchase tax deductions to reduce the tax bill.

6. *A rental property has positive cash flow, and taxes paid are high.* The positive cash flow is compounding the tax problem.

7. *There is insurance cash value and a substantial net worth.* There comes a time when the need for insurance ceases because the net worth has risen high enough.

8. *There is no pension plan.* A pension contribution is an easy and beneficial income tax deduction, and there would have to be a good reason why it was not taken.

9. *There is excess savings.* We will examine later why any savings may be excessive. Savings is an under-utilization of funds and must be kept to a minimum. Savings yields interest, which is taxable surplus (above a small minimum) and should be avoided.

10. *There are stock investments, and taxes are being paid.* Since stocks can be owned by a pension plan that does not have tax consequences when stocks are bought and sold, it would be unusual for an individual to own stocks in his own name.

11. *The net worth is under $1 million and the leverage ratio is low.* In an inflationary economy, you are not going to make money unless you borrow money.
If you want to be a millionaire, acquire $1 million of assets, whether they are paid for or not.

12. *The gross earnings are low.* Yes, this is a problem! Perhaps some family members are not using their time and talents to optimum capacity. Earnings have to be sufficient to cover tithing, subsistence, and a *provision for the future.*

13. *Income taxes paid are high.*
Over $10,000 a year is high!
Over $5,000 a year is high!
Much less is acceptable!
Between zero and $4-5,000 a year is permissible. In some cases zero is a very realistic goal.

14. *There is material capital gain in an asset.* A major capital gain can be a ticking time bomb, and the asset may need to be broken down into smaller assets.

15. *Notes receivable are high, and income tax paid is high.* The notes yield interest that is compounding the tax problem.

16. *There is too much equity in any one asset.* "Too much" could be defined as equity in excess of one year's earnings. This can cause a liquidity problem.

17. *Only purchases have been made.* Buying is one decision. It is equally important to know when to sell, refinance, or exchange. Assets outlive their usefulness, and benefits get used up.

18. *Taxpayers do not own a single family home.* Since they are taxpayers, they are not using one of the best income tax deductions available, the benefits of property ownership.
They do not necessarily have to live in the home; they can use it as rental property.

19. *There are not enough assets riding with inflation.* Single family homes do, treasury bills do not.

20. *There is limited or no diversification or liquidity.* All net worth statements must contain diversification and liquidity.

21.*There are assets with no known value.* People may have moved out of state and still own land, or they may have inherited property many miles away. Or they may have substantial family silver or jewelry in their own vault. It is not uncommon for people to overlook valuable assets.

22. *Wrong assets are held.* Bare land (builders and developers make the profit here), commercial buildings, inherited stocks—there are many examples of wrong assets to be found in any given individual portfolio.

Now that reasons to make a change have been defined in the personal net worth statement, let us examine the two problems facing everyone today. They are inflation and income taxes.

CHAPTER 5

Inflation

KNOW WHAT INFLATION IS

What is inflation? This is where you should spend some of your time on personal money management. If you do not know what inflation is and how it is caused, go to the library and get a good book on the subject so that you have a clear understanding of what it is and how long you think it will continue.

PENNY POSTCARD

In 1951 we could mail the preprinted postcard for one cent. That was only thirty-odd years ago and in the lifetimes of most of the readers of this book. After that the sequence was this:

1951	1 cent
1958	2 cents
1963	3 cents
1968	4 cents

After 1968, inflation really ran rampant, and 1968 is the start of the inflation rates we know today. The sequence continued:

1971	5 cents
1974	6 cents

And so it has continued, going up to 13 cents at this writing. Exactly the same goods and services have increased thirteen-fold in my lifetime.

Is inflation going to stop? The government doesn't think so. In fact, we notice that often they do not put the price on the stamps any more! They either cannot keep up with the price increases, or they would rather disguise how much they have increased.

BELIEF IN INFLATION

The following questions need to be answered by each individual.

Do we have inflation now?
Will we have inflation next year?
Will we have inflation the year after that?

That is as far as you have to look ahead. If you answer in the affirmative to those questions, you have to take protective action with your personal money management.

The same belief in inflation can be achieved in reverse. Do you seriously think there will be a day in the future when

gasoline is 25 cents a gallon?
first-class postage is 15 cents?
a cup of coffee is a quarter?

Again, if you cannot see those events taking place, you firmly believe in inflation and you have to do something about it.

Any rate of inflation is bad news. Do not be misled by media reports that the rate of inflation has been reduced. If there is inflation at all, proper defensive action must be taken in personal money management.

PURCHASING POWER OF THE DOLLAR

We have seen the following table published over the years. In this table, the dollar is pegged at 100 cents in 1967.

PURCHASING POWER OF THE DOLLAR SINCE 1940*

(1967 = $1.00)

Year	Value of the Dollar via Consumer Price Index
1940-44	2.38 (1940)
1945-49	1.85 (1945)
1950	1.39
1951	1.28
1952	1.26
1953	1.25
1954	1.24
1955	1.25
1956	1.23
1957	1.19
1958	1.16
1959	1.14
1960	1.13
1961	1.12
1962	1.10
1963	1.09
1964	1.08
1965	1.06
1966	1.03
1967	1.00
1968	.96
1969	.91
1970	.86
1971	.82
1972	.80
1973	.75
1974	.68
1975	.62
1976	.59
1977	.55
1978	.51
1979	.46
1980	.41

* *U.S. Department of Labor, Bureau of Labor Statistics, Handbook of Labor Statistics.*

If we had to forecast what the future trend will be three, five or ten years ahead, is it reasonable to think that the figures will turn up again? Will the numbers reverse and start climbing through 50 cents, 70 cents, and back up to $1? Again, if you don't think that will happen, you have to apply that belief in your personal money management. *You have to avoid cash and invest in items whose value increases with inflation.*

SAVINGS IN THE BANK

Let us consider the case of the couple who have their money in the bank. Unfortunately, we all know friends or relatives who still have their money in the bank and *think* they are earning 5¼ percent interest on their savings.

Applying what we have examined earlier, the interest on savings is the *last* income dollar. Since savings is discretionary and you can put that money wherever you want to, it is the interest that is added to the rest of the earnings. That makes the savings interest subjected to the *highest* tax rate. Since most taxpayers are around the 50 percent bracket—in many states, above the $35,000 level of taxable income will put taxpayers in the 50 percent bracket—we will compute the actual return over a full year using the 50 percent tax rate.

Interest on savings	5¼%
less income taxes	(2⅝%)
	2⅝%
less annual inflation	(10%)
True return on savings	− 7⅜%

Instead of *gaining* 5¼ percent on their investment, they are actually *losing* 7⅜ percent.

Many taxpayers over the last few years have realized that this was happening and have transferred their savings into other interest-bearing items such as money market funds or Treasury bills. They *think* they are better off. But you are not better off if all you are doing is losing less. Here could be their position.

Interest	16%
less income taxes	(8%)
	8%
less annual inflation	(10%)
True return	– 2%

If your money is earning interest, you are going backward because of inflation and taxes.

BANKS

Most people think of a bank as a deposit institution, a place to put your money. But what would happen to a bank if all it got was deposits? It would go broke. A bank must also lend money.

Since the days of high inflation began, we have seen a dramatic increase in the availability of consumer credit. Credit cards are commonplace. Bankers will also lend money to customers unsecured.

Many Christians have not taken advantage of those changes. Their parents taught them that borrowing was bad. They construe the use of credit cards and buying on credit as being against religious beliefs.

Coveting material items you cannot afford and do not really need is indeed a sin. "For where your treasure is, there will your heart be also" (Matt. 6:21). And credit is easily misused. Many of us have trouble controlling our spending when we can get what we want now just by presenting a piece of plastic.

Yes, the misuse of credit cards *is* wrong. But the *proper* use of credit and credit cards indicates that a Christian is keeping up-to-date and using a major technological advance to assist him in proper stewardship. So use credit wisely and carefully, but do take advantage of the benefits it provides.

NEGATIVE SAVINGS

To understand the proper use of credit, let us re-examine what we understand savings to be.

Savings is money that is in the bank.
It is money that you have set aside in case you need it.
It is money that is there for a rainy day.

It follows, then, that *credit is savings*—negative savings, if you prefer that term. Having credit available is the same as having savings in the bank.

If we have taken the trouble to build the proper relationship with the bank manager over a period of years and have demonstrated that we are good, responsible homeowners with stable employment, the manager will be only too delighted to lend us $5,000 on an unsecured basis.

Compare that *ability* to borrow with the definition of savings.

> The $5,000 is *money in the bank.*
> The $5,000 is there *in case we need it.*
> The $5,000 is there *for a rainy day.*

The same reasoning applies to credit cards. They represent the *ability* to obtain cash, goods, or services when required. *They take the place of savings.* Rather than having savings causing us damage by being eroded by taxes and inflation, this savings has to be out there working.

That is what the Bible says.

The holder of one talent was told in Jesus' parable that the very least that should have been done instead of burying the talent was to "put my money to the exchangers, and then at my coming I should have received mine own with usury" (Matt. 25:27).

Savings then as now is the *least-best* alternative. The best alternative, in those days as well as now, is that the money should be out there working and multiplying.

CREDIT CARDS

Credit cards help to build a strong defense in personal money management. Many cards can be obtained free of charge. It would be surprising if everyone did not have, for example, a Sears charge card. Sears is not only the world's biggest retailer, but it has also expanded into other financial markets with the acquisition of a major New York stock brokerage-investment firm. It seems likely that if Sears or its subsidiaries eventually offer new benefits or programs, they would first be made available to their cardholder customers. Possession of a Sears credit card at the very least may be a way to keep up with trends in the financial supermarkets of the future. Other major store credit cards should also be obtained free of charge.

American Express is one of the credit cards that costs money. However, it is the best administered and consequently provides the best credit reference for a cardholder. So from that perspective, a good case can be made for owning an American Express card. Mastercard and Visa also cost money to use but are most useful for their wide distribution and their flexibility in turning them into goods or cash.

It would be unusual for a taxpayer earning over $15,000 a year not to have accumulated at least that sum in negative savings (credit lines) from the systematic development of banking relationships and acquisition of credit cards over a period of years.

One major use of credit cards is their assistance in personal record-keeping. Any good record-keeping system will separate payments for personal items from payments for tax deductible items. Credit cards can be used to collect the payments of different types. For example, a Mastercard can be used for personal items and the Visa card for business or deductible items. The card's monthly statement provides a useful, detailed list of the transactions made. Keep in mind, however, that *credit card statements must be paid in full before the due date. It is not good stewardship to incur the interest charges for late or extended payments.* Beware of the danger of running up charge-account debts you cannot pay off when the bill comes.

DISASTER

Even in the best-managed and most-upright households, there are calamities that occur to test our faith. ("The trying of your faith worketh patience" [James1:13].) Four types come to mind that can happen to anyone at any time

    loss of job
    loss of good health through sickness or accident
    loss of spouse through death or divorce
    bad business decision.

Let's consider each of those briefly.

Loss of job

No matter how good and faithful the employee, corporate mergers, acquisitions, and bankruptcies are a fact of business life. There can be a period of several months or longer during which a person is unable to secure the right employment. To be prepared for such a possibility, good liquid investments and the availability of credit have to be established while one is employed.

Loss of good health through sickness or accident

Medical and disability insurance are a wise precaution for any family, but they alone will not offset the financial disruption that can be caused by a long illness. It is also difficult to find the time and mental concentration necessary to implement and maintain good personal money management if a person is not in the best of health.

Loss of spouse through death or divorce

Marital harmony is an essential ingredient in a good investment program. No long-term investments should be made unless there is total family unity. That may sound crass, and marital harmony is obviously desirable for more important reasons than just the stability of one's investment program, but it is true nonetheless.

Bad business decision

Bad business decisions occur more often than people realize. For that reason, flexibility and liquidity are vital features of an investment portfolio. You want to have as many alternatives available as possible in case any one investment turns sour.

The potential for a setback is always present. But that is not a reason to sit back and do nothing. On the contrary, it emphasizes that the proper investments must be made when earnings and the household are stable so that there is something to fall back on if unforeseen events occur.

The Bible says it this way: "There is that scattereth, and yet increaseth; and there is that withholdeth more than is meet, but it tendeth to poverty" (Prov. 11:24).

I don't know if we would want to be known as "scatterers"—maybe stewards is a better term. But certainly we must be active rather than passive investors.

Coupled with inflation, income taxes are the other all-pervasive item facing all households. Let us now consider the solution to the tax burden.

CHAPTER 6

Income Taxes

And the chief priests and the scribes the same hour sought to lay hands on him; and they feared the people: for they perceived that he had spoken this parable against them.

And they watched him, and sent forth spies, which should feign themselves just men, that they might take hold of his words, that so they might deliver him unto the power and authority of the governor.

And they asked him, saying, Master, we know that thou sayest and teachest... the way of God truly:

Is it lawful for us to give tribute unto Caesar, or no?

But he perceived their craftiness, and said unto them, Why tempt ye me?

Show me a penny. Whose image and superscription hath it? They answered and said, Caesar's.

And he said unto them, Render therefore unto Caesar the things which be Caesar's, and unto God the things which be God's.

And they could not take hold of his words before the people: and they marvelled at his answer, and held their peace [Luke 10:19-26].

Then as now, we have to differentiate between what is the government's and what is God's. If you, the taxpayer, have the option of how much you pay in taxes, you should exercise that option as a good Christian steward.

SOURCE OF TAX PROBLEM

Why is income tax such a difficult and misunderstood subject for most people? One reason is that income tax comes up only once a year, around April 15. Anything that comes up only once a year we are totally ill-equipped to handle. How would it be if we only went to church once a year? Played tennis once a year? Would we know the subject, be proficient at it? Then how are we supposed to do a competent job on our income taxes if they only come up once a year?

The second problem is that taxpayers have a "cannot win" attitude. They wonder how they can ever escape taxes without cheating. This attitude is also fostered by our religious teachings, where we frequently hear such statements as "It is inevitable just like death and taxes." One of those is inevitable, but the other certainly is not. Perhaps, unlike biblical times, there are ways to reduce taxes.

The third problem with income taxes is that the income tax return is written in very difficult and confusing English. What is essentially a simple addition and subtraction task has been transformed into a complicated, 84-page booklet with twists and turns and terms to confuse even the most clear-thinking participant.

If those are the background problems that most people encounter with income taxes, what are the solutions?

SOLUTIONS TO TAX PROBLEMS

The first solution is this: If you own anything other than your personal residence, any other investments whatsoever, you should employ the services of a C.P.A. to complete your tax return—one who specializes in income tax, and not any of the other tax preparers or relatives that many people use. If your child were sick, would you not want the best medical help available? With income taxes, too, you employ the best help there is. You may not need the full gamut of a C.P.A's professional expertise on a year-in, year-out basis, but if you are subjected to audit you need the best help available.

You must also recognize what the C.P.A. does. His function is to drop the numbers in the proper slots from the neat and tidy information you have prepared for him. *You, the taxpayer, however, have to know what your benefits are and go obtain them.* The C.P.A. can indicate to you that your tax bill is too high or that you need more deductions, but only you are equipped to find out about those deductions and apply them to your benefit.

Judge Learned Hand said it best: "Anyone may so arrange his affairs that his taxes shall be as low as possible; he is not bound to choose that pattern which best pays the treasury. Everyone does it, rich and poor alike, and all do right; for nobody owes any public duty to pay more than the law demands."

The second solution is that each taxpayer should keep aware of income taxes throughout the year and avoid the once-a-year occurrence. One way to do that is to read *The Wall Street Journal,* because each week there is a front-page column called "Tax Report." Reading that keeps you up-to-date and gives you ideas for your own tax return. The column does not just contain information for big corporations and people with a lot of money.

Each taxpayer should also have a good reference book to consult about tax-related items. Tax matters are misused and misquoted almost as often as the Bible is. One of the best reference books is an annual publication entitled the *U.S. Master Tax Guide.** That book is not obtainable from bookstores. The book is invaluable in helping taxpayers sort out their ideas before discussing items with their C.P.A.'s. The book will not explain how the tax system works; that is the next solution to the problem.

Each taxpayer should take a basic income tax course such as those put on by local community colleges and there obtain some understanding of the tax system and the opportunities available to not pay taxes.

WE DECIDE IF WE PAY TAXES

No good Christian steward should be paying a lot of taxes. It is that simple, in our opinion.

The government would have us believe that all our earnings really belong to it, but it allows us to keep most of the earnings and only remit a portion to it. That is not the case. We write our

---

* Commerce Clearing House, 4205 W. Peterson Ave., Chicago, IL 60646.

own ticket. We tell the government how much we owe—and then it has the right to challenge us. And we will only owe taxes if we have not taken the time and trouble to find enough deductions.

It is only the weak who leave their money in financial institutions for the financial institutions to reinvest or send taxes to the Government.

What does the government do with the taxes we send to Washington? We all know it redistributes them in different federal programs such as public assistance, defense, agriculture, housing, and many others.

What is not known and appreciated by the vast majority of taxpayers is that the government gives each individual bearing a Social Security number the right to choose some of those programs. If you select one of the approved programs you do not have to send your money to Washington but instead you may send (or invest) the money directly in that program.

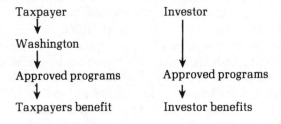

We all know this is the case because we see it illustrated clearly with our tithes and church offerings. We could send those funds to the federal government and have it redistribute them over all religious denominations. That does not happen, and wisely so. The government says to each taxpayer, "If you make a tithe or church offering, we will classify it as a charitable contribution and you can pay it directly to the church of your choice. If you do this we will reduce the taxes you owe us." Now, of course, the taxes are not reduced dollar for dollar, and the ratio varies for each individual.

The point is that this same pattern of reducing taxes can be continued, and we as taxpayers can even make those payments into programs that *will increase our personal wealth*. Now, would you rather pay a lot of taxes to the government or increase your personal wealth?

Buying a house and setting up a pension plan are two well-known programs that result in a reduction of income taxes and increase our personal wealth. We all know this, but now we have to find out how to follow through with this principle so that much of our tax bill is eliminated. That would be the mark of real Christian stewardship. Further explanations are necessary.

What Is Income Tax?

What is income tax? It is income minus deductions, which yields "taxable income." You then consult a tax table to see how much tax you pay on that taxable income.

Income for most of us is our earnings, be they from wages or salary, or business, and it is under our control. *But deductions are also under our control.*

You may strive hard to get your earnings up to $35,000, but you are not necessarily any better off than the person earning $25,000 who took the time to find out how to wipe out his tax bill. Consider what might happen:

Income	35,000	25,000
Taxes paid	(10,000)	—
Net income	25,000	25,000

The tax rates were examined earlier, and it was found that the tax bill could be reduced dramatically if the taxable income were reduced. There is another major benefit in rates that has to be explained.

Ordinary Income Versus Capital Gains

The IRS recognizes two different kinds of income. Ordinary income (which includes wages, salaries, interest, dividends, and others) is distinguished from capital gains. A capital gain is achieved if an item is bought and later sold at a profit. The profit is the gain. Yes, the IRS also recognizes and rewards those who multiply their talents!

Ordinary income is taxed according to the tax tables already examined, but with capital gains, *60 percent* of the gain is not taxed at all.* Only the balance of 40 percent* is taxed at ordinary income rates. Is that a benefit? Of course it is.

---

* This is the rate fixed by law at the time of this writing.

In other words, to gain from this tax advantage, you would avoid items that would add ordinary income—interest and dividends are the common ones here—and you would concentrate on items that would result in capital gain—stocks and real estate are common examples here.

Take as an example of the capital gains benefit the servant in the parable in Matthew 25 who parlayed five talents into ten. Would it be more beneficial under today's tax laws to have done it through usury (interest) or by investing (capital gains)? Let's compare the two, figuring one talent to be worth $10,000 and remembering that the servant made a profit of five talents.

Ordinary income		
less interest =	$50,000	Capital gain = $50,000
		40% taxable = 36,000
Federal taxes paid =	11,368	Federal taxes paid = 2,461

Would you rather pay $11,000 or $2,000 in taxes?

We know that if the servant were alive today, being as astute as he was, he would have invested for capital gain and not ordinary income. We'll return to this servant later and find out what other action he took so that he did not even have to pay the $2,461 tax bill.

A family can normally live off their income. Granted they may need every last penny of their income, but they can get by on their earnings. When that income increases, possibly from a pay raise, there is a short period of time when the raise may result in excess funds, but quite soon the family's lifestyle will have risen to the new earning level. There's nothing wrong with that. What it does mean, though, is that a family does *not* need to add to their income from outside sources, such as savings interest, to put bread and butter on the table. They *can* avoid additional ordinary income and they *should*, because that is what is increasing their tax bill.

To put it another way, 60 percent forgiven is a major break. If the government is giving taxpayers a benefit, *go and get the benefit*.

You and I both know how many people avoid that simple money-making principle. They are victims of those financial institution advertisements, and they chase the alleged 1 percent higher interest, the electric toaster, or the free-coffee-and-doughnut come-on. *Avoid adding to ordinary income. Seek capital gain.*

TAX PLANNING

There is a very simple test to differentiate between those who know about income taxes and are in control of the subject and those who allow taxes to control them. When do you draft your tax return? Those who draft their tax return *before* the end of the year, preferably in November, pass the test. The reason is that there are several decisions each taxpayer can make at the year's end that will determine what the final tax bill will be.

A prudent taxpayer will go even further than that, however. The tax return will be drafted *before the year starts.* Taxes are a controllable expense. A corporation prepares budgets and forecasts income and expenses for the year ahead, and you are in business just like a corporation. Here is the sequence to be followed for a 1984 income tax return that reports earnings and other transactions from January to December 1984.

First draft	November 1983
Second draft	November 1984
Completed and filed	April 1985

TAX REFUNDS

With the institution of withholding taxes from paychecks, and the requirement that self-employed people pay quarterly, the government made sure that most taxpayers pay more than what is due. The problem is that many taxpayers have too much tax taken out of their paychecks and end up with a refund. Seventy-five percent of people filing tax returns get a refund.

What justification is there for paying the government in advance? Why do people give the government free use of their money? Many people even think that if they got a refund they did not pay taxes! They do not realize that if the refund is set against the total taxes withheld from the paycheck during the year, the government always comes out a net winner.

This again bears out the incredible lack of knowledge people have about income taxes. In inflationary times, it just is not prudent money management to give the government an interest-free loan.

Worse yet, some people consider the overwithholding of income tax a form of saving. But that is the worst possible kind of savings. The government gives you no interest on the money.

W-4

The W-4 is the form an employee completes to authorize an employer to deduct income taxes from the paycheck. Depending on the number of allowances claimed, the payroll department consults a set of tables and takes out taxes accordingly. The higher the number of allowances, the less tax is taken out. Most employees are familiar with that procedure.

What many employees are not familiar with is that the W-4 does not just have to show the number of dependents. If an employee has rigorously pursued and obtained deductions, the number of allowances claimed on the W-4 form may be increased and less taxes will be taken out of the check. That can be done at any time during the year.

There has been some misuse of this instruction, and the IRS may ask for supporting information on anyone claiming more than fourteen allowances. That does not mean it is wrong to claim more than fourteen; it only means you may have to justify it. The IRS is quite clear in its instructions that it is up to the taxpayer to adjust the amount withheld from paychecks so that the final over or underpayment that appears on the tax return is minimal.

Whenever you make an investment that increases your deductions, remember to change your W-4 form. That additional sum in each paycheck may help you pay for the investment.

CHAPTER 7

Tithing or Taxes?
Common Income Tax Deductions

Question—tithing or taxes; or tithing and taxes?

Wouldn't life be easier if you only had to tithe and not pay as many taxes? We have already seen how a reduction in the taxable income reduces the tax bill. Let us now study some of the more common income tax deductons and examine the flexibility of a taxpayer to pick and choose between them to his own personal advantage.

TITHING

Tithing is an excellent income tax deduction and gives the taxpayer the opportunity to make a positive statement about both the church and taxes. Ten percent from the top of the gross income is a small sum to pay when it is compared with the 20, 30, or 40 percent and more that the government extracts from most paychecks. Other church offerings and charitable donations are also good income tax deductions.

INTEREST

Interest paid on a house mortgage is also an excellent income tax deduction. We will examine later the reasons for owning your own personal residence and the investment advantages it provides, but for tax purposes, making a house payment has all the benefits over making a rental payment.

A $500 a month rent payment is the same net out of pocket to a taxpayer as a $1,000 a month house payment ($1000 payment less $500 tax savings, if in the 50 percent tax bracket).

INDIVIDUAL PENSION PLAN—IRA OR KEOGH

The 1981 income tax act liberalized the benefits for a taxpayer setting up his own pension plan. The deduction allowed for a contribution to an IRA or Keogh plan is now available to all taxpayers and should be taken advantage of. The fact that IRA and Keogh investments are allowed to compound tax-deferred should by now be understood by readers to be a major benefit. It means that the income from such accounts is not added to other income *at the highest tax rate*. The ability to wheel and deal with an investment and have no tax consequences until the money is finally withdrawn is the finest benefit that could be written into any tax package, and it must not be ignored by investors.

NON-CASH DEDUCTIONS

The income tax deductions that have been discussed until now are cash deductions. One dollar paid equals one dollar of deduction. But it is also possible to get income tax deductions for non-cash transactions. Two of the best known are charitable donations and depreciation.

Charitable donations

Donation of goods to a recognized charity—church bazaar, Salvation Army, Goodwill—is an easy deduction for any family. Used personal effects should never be thrown in the garbage. They may have outlived their usefulness for the family, but they may still have years of use for others. Record-keeping, again, is the key here. A detailed description of the items donated and a receipt for the property are the minimum that is required. This is a good example of where the taxpayer would refer to the *U.S. Master Tax Guide* to find what the IRS allows in this regard.

Since the taxpayer can determine when the goods are donated, this is one of the instances where a taxpayer can control taxable income from one year to the other.

Depreciation

One of the most lucrative of all income tax deductions is depreciation. The IRS allows taxpayers to write off the value of a piece of improved property (other than personal residence) over a number of years to offset the supposedly decreasing value of the property. However, you and I know that in most cases, because of inflation, a property does not depreciate in value. Rather, it tends to appreciate. A taxpayer, therefore, gets the double benefit of increasing personal net worth and decreasing taxes. That sounds like good stewardship.

For example:

Rental house bought for	$100,000
less land	25,000
Building value	75,000
Depreciate over 15 years	= 5,000 per year

This fifteen years of depreciation came in with the 1981 tax act and is of great benefit to taxpayers. It is also possible to take 175 percent of that figure, if desired, under the rules for accelerated depreciation, so here again is a deduction that the taxpayer can control to good advantage.

NEGATIVE CASH FLOW

The ownership of rental property has other important advantages. Leverage is one of them. It does not take $100,000 cash to get title to $100,000 of rental property. The taxpayer can decide how much cash to put down on that property, and the balance can be in mortgages, either from a financial institution or from the seller.

Since the taxpayer can control the cash down payment, the taxpayer can also control the cash flow on the property (cash flow being the difference between rent and other receipts and the total costs of ownership, such as principal, interest, property taxes, insurance, repairs, and management).

As an example, let us take $100,000 of rental property and finance it three different ways. That figure is used because it can be readily adjusted by taxpayers to suit their own areas. In some parts of the country, $100,000 could be the combined market value of two or even three rental properties; in other parts it would not equal one.

	A	B	C
Rental property market value	$100,000	$100,000	$100,000
Loans	(60,000)	(70,000)	(80,000)
Cash down payment	40,000	30,000	20,000
Cash flow	Positive	Breakeven	Negative

Which one would a taxpayer choose? Because the word *taxpayer* has been used, defined as an individual who pays taxes, we would never want to be in position A. A positive cash flow adds to taxable income and is compounding the tax problem. A taxpayer could choose to be in position B, but better still in position C. In C, the combined effects of the negative cash flow plus depreciation will drastically reduce the taxes paid.

Do not be concerned at this stage with that common question, "Yes, but how do I pay for it?" Remember, it is the systematic piecing together of all this information that will identify a good Christian steward. Many people, when told that a property rents out for $300 a month and the total costs of ownership are $500 a month, say they cannot afford it. They do not realize that it is only one piece of the puzzle, and perhaps the benefits to be derived from the other pieces will more than offset the apparent negative cash flow. Specific examples of how all this is put together will be examined in the case studies in the next-to-last chapter.

INADVISABLE DEDUCTIONS

Let us now look at two common deductions that are frequently discussed but that may not be advisable for taxpayers to use.

Use of part of the home as an office

Several years ago, this was a favorite ploy for taxpayers. If they could demonstrate that a portion of their residence was used on a regular basis to support their regular, income-producing work, they allocated some of the costs to that section of the house and got a deduction on their tax returns. Teachers, supervisors, engineers, salespeople— everyone did it if they took work home with them.

A few years ago, the IRS decided to tighten the rules in this area. It laid out specific requirements governing when the deduction would be allowed, and it stringently set out to enforce those rules.

There was also another side-effect to the deduction that many people had not considered. When a portion of the residence was called the office, the sale of that residence did not allow 100% participation in the lucrative benefits available to a taxpayer on the sale of a personal residence.

The combined effect of those two facts makes a deduction for using one's home part-time for business purposes a bad decision.

Incorporating

A favorite tactic for several people who have increasing incomes, and who are in a position to do so, is to incorporate. They regularly cite three benefits from incorporating.

limited liability
better pension and medical deductions
lower tax rates

Those benefits can be obtained, but you have to look beyond that. Any taxpayer now has good pension benefits available with the new IRA and Keogh provisions, but a pension plan does not contribute to the overall liquidity of the taxpayer. A balance has to be achieved between having access to funds in an investment and a better tax deduction.

The main reason many people incorporate is for lower tax rates. Great! We have already seen that personal income tax rates of 30, 40, and 50 percent are indeed high, but the lowest corporate tax rate in many states is around 20 percent (federal and state combined). Now does it make sense to pay 20 percent of your profits in taxes? Twenty percent is an enormous penalty just because people have not taken the time and effort to secure personal income tax deductions in their own name.

For *some* people with consistently high incomes above

$50,000 a year, incorporating *may* be good tax strategy. For the majority of people who incorporate, it is not.

INCOME AVERAGING

Did you know that the IRS substantially rewards with a handsome bonus those diligent stewards who consistently paid little or no taxes for several years in a row? It does not appear in the IRS code in just those terms, but it has the same effect.

Income averaging, as you may know, is a means whereby a taxpayer with rapidly increasing or erratic income can average out the incomes over a certain number of years and get the benefits of lower income tax rates. Students of taxation, in learning about this concept, are frequently given an author as the taxpayer illustrated. The author may go for one or two years with low output and earnings and then suddenly write a best seller. The high earnings year can be combined with the earnings of the previous four years, which has the effect of substantially reducing the tax rates and the taxes subsequently paid.

This principle can also work to the advantage of the good Christian steward who has control of his taxes. Let us assume that even with rapidly increasing income, deductions were obtained to offset this as follows:

	Year 1	Year 2	Year 3	Year 4
Total income	20,000	30,000	50,000	70,000
Deductions	20,000	30,000	50,000	70,000

In year 5, if the taxpayer's income jumped to $100,000 but by some mischance deductions were zero, taxes would not be levied on the $100,000. Income averaging dictates that the combined taxable income of the five years can be averaged. Four years of zero taxable income with one year of $100,000 taxable income means that the taxpayer would only have to pay taxes at the $20,000 level for the fifth year rather than the $100,000 level—a substantial reduction or reward for diligence.

DECEMBER 31 IS A FIXED DATE

December 31 is the date of our report card to the IRS. Any financial event in the twelve months prior has to be reported to it.

That last date in the year can come up very quickly for those who have tax problems. Just as income does not necessarily flow in regularly throughout the year, several deductions are also prorated over the year. That is why forward planning is so important in income taxes.

The time to consider the total financial implications, including tax consequences, of a transaction is *before* any action is taken on the event

> before the personal residence is listed for sale
> before you change employment
> before you add on to your house
> before you give away an asset or a portion thereof
> before you consider the sale or transfer of real
>   estate, stocks, or other major assets
> before the end of November

NUMBER ONE SERVANT'S TAX RETURN

Let us return to the example used in the previous chapter from the parable of the talents and see how number one servant adapted our tax rules to his advantage. Here is what may have happened.

The astute servant made sure that his appointment to report back to his master was made early in the year so that when he had to cash in the investments, there would be all year to find deductions to cover the gain.

The servant received one additional talent as a bonus and would be only too pleased to tithe his full 10 percent or $6,000. That would be a valuable income tax deduction to set against the large capital gain incurred—he had made 100 percent profit on his investment.

Taking advantage of the new depreciation provisions, the servant calculated that a breakeven position in the ownership of one rental house and a negative cash flow on the other would be needed to help offset the gain.

Using the information gleaned from this book, properties A & B were selected with this profile:

	A	B
Rental market value	100,000	100,000
Loans	80,000	70,000
Cash down payment	20,000	30,000
Cash flow	Negative	Breakeven

One of each of these houses was purchased for a total of $50,000 downpayment, leaving $4,000 to pay for the negative cash flow. Each house would yield $5,000 in depreciation.

It could work like this:

Profit		$50,000
Additional gift		10,000
		60,000
Less tithe		6,000
Available to invest		54,000
Capital gain 40% of 50,000		$20,000
Less tithe 6,000		
Depreciation	10,000	
Negative cash flow	4,000	20,000
Taxable income		ZERO
Taxes to be paid		ZERO

Paying no taxes can be done and our hero has $200,000 of good rental property that will yield future depreciation deductions to offset the profits of future trading ventures.

(Note: poetic license has been taken in this example to illustrate a point. In practice there would be a minimum preference tax payable.)

Why was real estate selected? What other investment vehicles were available? We shall now examine the full range if investments and decisions that should be made to indicate which ones are selected.

CHAPTER 8

Investment Alternatives

Where do you invest? This is the area of greatest confusion for most people, and yet the number of major investment vehicles is small. Once the vehicle has been selected, there is an infinite number of alternatives within that vehicle. However, if the principles of investing and improving net worth are clearly understood, it becomes quite easy to pick the specific investment.

Inflation and income tax are the two dominant items that influence any investment decision. Liquidity is another, but this has already been taken care of with the proper use of negative savings. The remaining item is diversification.

You have to diversify. "Give a portion to seven, and also to eight; for thou knowest not what evil shall be upon the earth" (Eccles. 11:2). We do not know what is going to happen in the future. Things change, and change quickly. There are no sure-fire ways to invest and automatically reap a profit anymore. For about thirty years prior to 1966, the stock market had a general upward trend and was probably the best place to put your money. Gold, on the other hand, was fixed at $35 an ounce and would have been the poorest choice. Since 1966, these investments have done an about-face. The stock market has been in the doldrums, and gold has increased in value ten or twenty times.

71

How does the average individual know when is the right time to buy one item and not another? You don't—and probably never will!

Thus, you cannot put all your eggs in one basket. You have to diversify over as many investment vehicles as possible, and also diversify within a given vehicle itself. You cannot buy just stocks or real estate or leave your money earning interest. You may have to participate in all three for different reasons.

Keep, then, at the back of your mind,
 inflation
 income tax
 liquidity
 diversification
and let us consider the investment vehicles.

The major investment vehicles are seven in number and are
 money instruments
 insurance
 stocks, bonds, commodities
 real estate
 small business
 gold, silver, and precious stones
 paying hobbies, collectibles

MONEY INSTRUMENTS

A money instrument is any type of deposit that yields interest—savings accounts, treasury bills, money market funds, second trust deeds, and the like. We have already examined why, because of inflation and income taxes, a money instrument is an unwise investment choice *regardless* of the interest rate. Although it is a bad choice for investment, some form of money instruments would be the temporary parking place for funds that were being accumulated for future investment. As a temporary parking place, money market funds are probably the best vehicle, as they offer competitive interest rates and liquidity.

When you get down to selecting a money market fund from the dozens available, stick with name brands. Go on the principle that the biggest is the best. If the biggest has got investment conditions you cannot meet, go on to the second biggest and so on down the line. You as an individual cannot be expected to pick winners each time, and you should not even try. What you need is a competitive interest rate.

Don't overlook the ability within a family to combine funds to secure a better interest rate. Parents frequently open savings accounts for children to teach them thrift, and the funds compound at 5¼% until the children become adults and realize the mistake made. Why not also teach the children syndication at the same time? There could be an older relative, such as a grandparent, who would also like the advantage of higher interest rates. A combination of two or more of these people can often double the interest received by each individual.

Such a joint approach also helps the child learn and appreciate what has been called "The Eighth Wonder of the World"—compounding. Compounding is where money earns money. Many people have overlooked or forgotten the basic principles of thrift, where money added on a regular basis to a fund earning interest at a competitive rate in ten years or more grows into an enormous sum because of compounding.

To recapitulate, savings may be a good place to learn these important principles:

> thrift
> syndication
> compounding

But no form of money instrument is a good place to invest money for the long term.

INSURANCE

Some form of medical and disability insurance is a must for a family at all times. This often comes through an employer's benefit program. There are also times when a family should carry some form of life insurance. Let it also be said that most of the time, a good Christian steward does not need life insurance. That is, of course, contrary to what the insurance companies would have us believe.

Life insurance is not a good investment. It is not a way to

increase or protect net worth. It is a way to protect the earnings if something should happen to the breadwinner. The tremendous emancipation of women over recent years and their ability to earn has made obsolete a lot of the former reasons for life insurance. At the other end of the scale, the proper selection of investments and the relaxing of the laws on inheritance taxes have virtually eliminated the necessity to carry life insurance as an instant source of funds on death.

A certain amount of life insurance may be necessary when there are young children and a low net worth, but the insurance should be dropped when those conditions change.

When do you need life insurance, and how much? At the regular quarterly review of the net worth statement, the following questions should be asked: "What would happen if one of us were not here?" "What sum of money would the other need, in addition to the present net worth and any employer or government benefits, to fulfill his obligations?"

I suggest that the answer to this second question is much less than the insurance companies would have us believe, and that this is the amount of insurance protection that should be purchased.

STOCKS, BONDS, AND COMMODITIES

Commodities can be eliminated quickly. This book is for people who have a net worth under $1 million, and those people should not be investing in commodities. Commodities are a high-risk, volatile investment for those who have the knowledge and the capital to pursue it.

On the other hand, you have to invest in stocks or bonds. The reason is simple. The setting up of a pension plan was identified as a great income tax deduction and a wise move for anyone wanting to increase his net worth. But where do you direct the trustee to invest the pension funds? On the stock market. Incidentally, many people are not aware that stocks can be bought with pension funds. That is because banks and savings and loans do the bulk of the advertising in this field, and they, of course, will only invest the funds within their own institutions. It is easy, however, to change the trustee. Find a trustee with wider investment powers, say in stocks and money market funds, give him the problem, and he can easily show you how to change trustees without tax consequences.

Because you have a pension fund, *because* you have to diversify, you have to invest on the stock market. Which stocks do you choose? Again, that is not too difficult if you define your objectives and seek good professional help. You are not looking for jackpots. You are not trying for riches overnight. This is a pension fund. You are looking for a good, steady return that will compound your funds tax-free and that is ahead of the rate of inflation.

There may be some industries or products that you have personal knowledge of, or there may be industries you can identify that are going to grow in importance in the future. Pick those out and discuss them and your objectives with a stock-broker.

How do you choose a stockbroker? How do you choose a doctor or a dentist? You go by personal referral. You choose one you can relate to and feel confident with. If you cease to have total confidence in your professional advisers, you should switch immediately.

Identify the growth you want from your pension fund over the next three to five years. You do this by selecting a return higher than you would achieve if you had to put your funds in one of today's competitive money instruments. If the going interest rate is 10 percent from a money market fund, you may select a 12-15 percent return on your stocks. A 13 percent money market interest rate may make your pension fund objective 16-22 percent.

Select your stockbroker, identify your goals, reach unanimity in your decisions, and go to it. Unanimity of decision will also dictate that only a few stocks are selected. If you feel strongly enough about a stock to purchase it, be willing to stake at least 10 percent of the funds in your belief. Since a pension plan is supposed to be conservative, it is difficult to imagine a situation in which more than 25 or 30 percent is in one individual stock (a fund under $5,000 may be in just one or two stocks). Many people have too many stocks, which is a mistake. The following is a good, general example of a pension plan:

Stock A	15%	3,000
B	20%	4,000
C	25%	5,000
D	25%	5,000
Cash	15%	3,000
	100%	20,000

No matter what recommendation or reasoning is advanced for investing in the stock market, there are people, either from prior experience or the unwillingness to learn, who refuse to invest there. Those who feel that way would invest their pension plan in high-yielding money instruments.

REAL ESTATE

The major investment vehicle for any family has to be real estate. It is the one investment with which you can use leverage plus counter inflation and income taxes.

You are never going to increase your net worth substantially while you have a major income tax drain. It does not make sense to try to accumulate money when you are needlessly throwing it away. Good investment strategy today suggests that real estate is the best investment in today's conditions.

The specific kind of real estate to choose and how and when it is purchased will be examined in the next two chapters. But for now we repeat that real estate will probably be the dominant item in any successful investment portfolio.

SMALL BUSINESS

Small business has to be identified as a separate investment vehicle. Small business would include any form of privately owned business, such as a beauty shop, engineering works, photography studio, or other entrepreneurial endeavor. It is very specialized and very risky. However, if you know what you are doing, it can produce a high return in both earnings and the accumulation of net worth.

Because a small business is such a high risk, it is not generally a prudent investment for anyone other than the owner-operator. There could, however, be situations within a family when family members provide some of the capital; but for most people there are many more profitable investments with less risk involved than investing in a small business.

For you who earn your living from your own small business, a couple of words of caution. It is doubly important that assets and investments are accumulated outside the business. This relates again to the need for diversification.

Being in business is difficult today. There is a myriad of government regulations to be observed, complex business principles to be learned, and an environment that is not under the control of the owner. Too many people put in their finest years laboring long and hard to build up a business, only to find that the business cannot be sold for enough to provide an adequate standard of retirement living. A business is not liquid. It is difficult to value, difficult to find a buyer for, and difficult to get your money out of.

Business is not static. There are good times and bad times. Most business people should start a business, build it up, and then either sell it or diversify into other investments bought by the business.

Many business owners would earn a higher return if they had to sell their businesses and deposit the proceeds in the bank. Too many businesses do not provide an adequate return for the owner's time and capital. Thus, as an investment to increase the net worth, small business is not the solution for most people.

GOLD, SILVER, PRECIOUS STONES

Gold, silver, and precious stones have been recognized symbols of wealth since biblical times. Maybe that tells us something. Maybe we should own them.

The answer is yes. Gold, silver, and precious stones can be a prudent investment at the right time and in the proper form and quantity. If your net worth exceeds $100,000, 5-10 percent of the net worth should be in gold, silver, or precious stones.

Why? Money is a medium of exchange, but just one of the media. Under certain conditions, gold, silver, and precious stones can also become media of exchange. Because of inflation, money decreases in value. Maybe these other tangible items do not depreciate in value, but increase.

Now, do not go rushing out to the nearest retail jeweler and purchase an expensive ornament. If you are not familiar with those products as an investment, read books, go to seminars. Remember, you did not know about real estate when you purchased your first residence.

Learn about them, get in the habit of buying a certain quantity of coins a year, one or two or five, whatever you are comfortable with. A systematic accumulation within the parameters mentioned will iron out the price fluctuation.

At the beginning, you can use precious metals and stones for personal adornment if you are comfortable doing that. Be sure to buy quality items that will not date too quickly with fashion changes. There comes a time when the regular accumulation will exceed the personal adornment requirements, and then they become investments.

Which do you choose? Remember the principles of liquidity and diversification and that these items are a medium of exchange. You select the items that can most easily be valued and have the highest number of potential buyers. For example, gold and silver prices are quoted daily in the financial pages. People tend to prefer either gold or silver. Those gold-oriented may select gold coins, whereas silver fanciers may accumulate silver-content American coins from 1964 and earlier.

The same idea applies to precious stones. Diamonds are the most universally accepted, but rubies, sapphires, emeralds, and so on may also provide fun and profit to the collector.

Again, at the right time and in the correct proportions, a sound investment portfolio today would include gold, silver, and precious stones.

PAYING HOBBIES, COLLECTIBLES

A paying hobby is the accumulation of a collectible that is periodically exchanged for cash or more collectibles. Stamps, coins, antiques, antique cars, rugs, tapestries, artwork, sculpture—the list is endless of the items people collect.

Collectibles are not usually included in the discussion of the accumulation of net worth. There is nothing wrong with collectibles whatsoever. They are good anti-inflationary items and good investments as long as you know what you are doing with them. But they do not get included in net worth as long as they remain under 10 percent of the total value of your assets. If their value is higher than 10 percent of the total, they become material and have to be included with other investments on the net worth statement, which is measured quarterly for leverage and appreciation.

OTHER INVESTMENT-TYPE PROGRAMS

Employer's benefit programs.   Many larger employers have investment-related benefit programs that employees can participate in if they wish. These benefit programs can range all the way from stock options and stock purchases to savings and pension plans and life insurance. In many cases, the corporation encourages the employees to participate by matching a portion of the employee's contribution. This matching can substantially increase the potential rate of return of the program.

This type of program represents a form of forced savings for the employee and is a relatively painless way to accumulate funds easily in a managed investment. Employees should investigate in detail what programs are available, and it would be surprising if they did not participate in those programs to the maximum allowed.

Partnerships.   Owning an investment in partnership with another taxpayer is not normally a wise move. Real estate is where this most frequently occcurs, where two or more may join together to make the down payment.

Income taxes are such an integral part of real estate ownership that it would be almost impossible to find someone with identical tax objectives. Coupled with that are the characteristics of flexibility and liquidity that an investment should have. Real estate is not normally considered a liquid investment, and when you add the fact of a partnership, it becomes even less liquid.

Many people enter into a partnership or real estate ownership looking only at reasons that make the purchase easier. They may think a little further ahead and consider the use of the partnership in managing the property. Seldom do they think it all the way through and look at the problems of disposing of the property. It is every bit as important to know when and how to dispose of property as it is to know when and how to buy it.

There are, on occasion, sound reasons for a real estate partnership. An older person may need a stake in inflation and join with a younger person who does most of the work. A parent may assist in getting a child started in real estate ownership.

Generally speaking, though, a real estate partnership ends up causing more problems than it was worth, and owning investments in partnership is to be discouraged.

Let us examine in more detail why real estate is the best investment vehicle for net worth accumulation and what particular kind of real estate should be purchased.

CHAPTER 9

Personal Residence

A person renting today is obtaining a product considerably under market price. Rents have not risen in proportion to property values over the last few years, and the vast majority of renters are being subsidized heavily by the landlords. Renting, therefore, would appear to be a wise decision. However, that is not the end of the story.

Renters have three major problems.

1. Renters are not in control of their own long-term housing costs.

2. Renters derive no income tax benefit from their shelter payment.

3. Renters have no stake in the inflationary spiral.

These three items combined dictate that renting should be abandoned and home ownership sought as soon as possible.

Let us qualify that statement slightly. It is a mistake for anyone to start out on net worth accumulation at too early an age. At the start of a career, all the emphasis has to be on developing experience and increasing the earnings. Many of life's experiences have to be sampled and enjoyed before a person is required to settle down to a more traditional and routine lifestyle. As a result, it would be unusual for single people to start trying aggressively to accumulate net worth under the age of 30. Below

30, if they have investment funds available, they can pick up useful experience by investing in money instruments, the stock market, and other more-liquid ventures. They would do this even recognizing that they may be overpaying in income taxes as a result. In inflationary times, net worth accumulation is not difficult once the principles are learned and a family has made the united decision to practice good Christian stewardship.

A married couple under that age, on the other hand, may have decided already on a more settled lifestyle, and a house purchase before 30 may be a wise investment for them.

PERSONAL RESIDENCE SINGLE BEST INVESTMENT

Once a decision is made to purchase a home, the first thing to consider is that the personal residence is the single best investment any family owns. That is true regardless of the size of the net worth. The reason is that the family lives there. A family is going to take care of its own home, so the house is not exposed to the risks that rental property may be exposed to.

The next principle is that the greater the asset value of the personal residence, the better. The sooner you can move from a $60,000 house into a $90,000 house the better, and from the $90,000 house into one worth $120,000, $150,000, and so on up to what is a prudent maximum to suit the needs and lifestyle of the family.

Why? Because a $120,000 house appreciates by twice as much as a $60,000 house. If the inflation rate is 10 percent, a $120,000 house may appreciate $12,000, whereas a $60,000 house may appreciate $6,000. Since the residence is the best investment vehicle for a family and we are in inflationary times, the higher the asset value a family can control, the better. Income taxes also come into play here. IRS regulations give certain benefits for replacing a residence after two years. This means that each time a quarterly net worth review is made, consideration has to be given to changing the personal residence.

The first consideration regarding the personal residence is mental. Mental considerations override and come prior to the financial considerations. The question that has to be answered is as follows: "Is this the best shape and location for the needs, wants, desires, and lifestyle of the family?" To this should be added a time frame, so the question has to be answered in relation to now and for the next three years. Things change. A couple starts a family, children grow up and leave home, yard-work loses its enchantment. What is adequate now may not be adequate later.

FINANCING

Because of inflation, interest rates tend to rise. If financial institutions provide more benefits to depositors, such as increased yields or interest on checking, the costs of the financial institutions rise. And if their costs go up, they in turn must charge more for money they lend out.

Granted, interest rates seem exorbitant today—but try waiting two or three years and see what they are. You do not have to be an economic genius and try to forecast interest rates. Interest rates are not the most important financial aspect of the house you want to finance. The total asset value is, as it is the value of the house that represents the stake you have in inflation.

The best long-term, fixed-rate (if possible) first mortgage has to be obtained from a lender. For those buying a new or replacement house, that means buyers have to come up with a cash down payment for the difference between the purchase price and the loan, or they can negotiate a further loan from the seller or another party. For those who have decided to stay in their existing residence, it means they are refinancing their house because they believe interest rates will go higher still and they realize some of the equity tied up in their home should be out in the marketplace working for them.

Having only a first mortgage against a personal residence is a mark of financial security. The goal of those who have a second or more mortgages against their personal residence would be to pay those off as soon as possible.

Many people think that because they have a low-fixed-interest mortgage against their personal residence, they have something valuable. That is not so. What is true is that they have a lot of equity that is not working for them, and they are not using one of the best income tax deductions available, a house payment with a lot of interest in it.

WHO IS BETTER OFF?

Who is better off in this example?

Mr. Stable Citizen is worth $75,000. His house is now valued at $100,000, and his loan has been paid down to $25,000. His annual income is $40,000, the same income as his neighbor Mr. Shrewd Steward.

Mr. Steward is also worth $75,000, but he refinanced his house and used the proceeds to purchase two rental properties. Here are some simple figures showing the relative financial postions of Mr. Citizen and Mr. Steward:

Mr. Stable Citizen's house	$100,000
Loan	(25,000)
Net worth	$ 75,000
Mr. Stable Citizen's simplified tax return	
Gross earnings	$ 40,000
Residence mortgage interest	3,000
Taxable income	37,000
Federal taxes thereon	8,025
Mr. Stable Citizen's take-home pay	$ 40,000
Less taxes	(8,025)
Take-home	$ 31,975
Mr. Shrewd Steward's house	$100,000
Loan	(75,000)
Rental house	100,000
Loan	(75,000)
Rental house	100,000
Loan	(75,000)
Net worth	$ 75,000
Mr. Shrewd Steward's simplified tax return	
Income	$ 40,000
Residence mortagage interest	9,000
Depreciation on rental houses ($5,000 x 2)	10,000
Negative cash flow on rental houses ($3,000 x 2)	6,000
Total deductions	25,000
Taxable income	15,000
Federal taxes	1,823

Mr. Shrewd Steward's take-home pay	$ 40,000
Less taxes	(1,823)
Negative cash flow on rental properties	(6,000)
Total deletions	(7,823)
Take-home	$ 32,177

Mr. Shrewd Steward not only takes home more money, even after subsidizing his rental properties, but he also controls *three times* as much property as Mr. Stable Citizen. Mr. Shrewd Steward will continue to be better off in the future, even if his real estate holdings go up, down, or sideways in value over the short term. That is because the rents will continue to increase, and that will improve his cash flow, as the major portion of his rental expenses is fixed.

BE AVAILABLE FOR BENEFITS

The Bible is full of stories in which Jesus was besieged and surrounded by people seeking help or cures. Why were they there in such great numbers? Jesus was dispensing benefits, and they wanted to be sure they were present and available when the benefits were being handed out.

That is easy enough for us to understand. And yet when the government provides excellent tax-savings benefits surrounding home ownership, many people head off in a different direction. Everything today is taxed. We make a profit, it is taxed. We earn money, it is taxed. Therefore, the greatest benefit available to anyone would be the ability to sell something and not pay taxes on the gain. That benefit is there—but you have to make yourself available and eligible to receive it.

The IRS says, "Sell your house and replace it with another, and we won't charge you taxes on any profit you made on the first house."

"Hold on," you say, "those taxes are not forgiven. They are just deferred, and you have to replace the house with a more expensive one."

You are correct, but it is still a major advantage to have the use of the government's money for such an extended period of time.

This means that you would *never* turn your residence into a rental. If you turn your residence into a rental, you have sidestepped the benefits. You no longer qualify for being able to sell the house and not pay taxes. This is explained in greater detail in chapter 11.

The IRS goes further and says, "Reach age 55, sell the residence you've lived in for three out of the last five years, and we will let you have $125,000 of the gain tax free!"

Is that a benefit? Of course it is. To be able to obtain a profit of $125,000 and not pay *any* taxes on that gain, is a most lucrative benefit. But it also means that you had better start out now to make sure you have $125,000 in accumulated profits in your existing personal residence by age 55.

If someone is handing out benefits, you must make yourself available to receive those benefits. That is good Christian stewardship. But some of you hedge and say, "Yes, but they may change the rules before we get there." That is a good example of non-Christian negative thinking, because the implication is that the rules would be changed to the detriment of the recipient. The opposite is true, in fact. The "old age" benefit described above has been on the books for many years and keeps changing *in favor of the taxpayer*. In recent years, we have seen the applicable age reduced to 55 and the amount increased to $125,000, so again there is an urgency to line yourself up for those benefits as soon as possible.

SECOND HOME

Some affluent families are in a position to purchase a second home. One of the best-known examples of this was the Kennedy compound off Cape Cod, where the large branches of the family could gather on vacations and major occasions. Several years ago there were income tax advantages in owning a second home. It was rented out when the family was not using it and was therefore given the benefits of rental property, such as depreciation.

Those rules have become much more stringent, however, and now only a relatively few days of annual use by family members make the house unavailable for the benefits of rental property.

OWN PROPERTY BUT DO NOT LIVE THERE

There are times and circumstances in which a family needs the benefit of investing in real estate but does not want to own a personal residence. Possibly they cannot afford it, even with the most imaginative financing. Living downtown in a major city, for example, may be prudent for reasons of employment but too expensive for home ownership. Employment requiring frequent travel may put a premium on mobility, which makes ownership of a personal residence too restrictive.

Those cases can sometimes be solved by joint ownership or continuing to rent and investing in rental property.

What kind of rental property should an investor look for and own? We'll consider that next.

CHAPTER 10

Why You Should Buy and Hold Single-Family Homes

Buy a Rental

The personal residence is the cornerstone of the net worth statement. Inflation and income tax dictate that in the early years of ownership, the residence should be changed and upgraded to a prudent maximum. And there comes a time after one of these changes has been made and a new residence has been bought and properly financed that there are surplus funds available for investment.

Where should those funds be invested? That may appear to be a difficult question requiring a detailed answer, but the answer is incredibly simple. Stay with what you know! If ownership of your personal residence proved to be a good investment, buy another single-family home. Don't live there, rent it out.

Just like any other solution that is so simple, most people overlook it. They will do anything else other than buying a rental, single-family home. Land, duplexes, apartments, commercial buildings, stocks, money market funds, gold—they will totally avoid the item they have had personal experience in as a sound and fruitful investment, and which they easily understand. They will head off in a different direction and completely ignore the item that yielded the profit to invest.

Stay with what you know! Buy a single-family home and rent it out.

BENEFITS

The government encourages the investment we are advocating. It provides benefits to investors. Go and get those benefits such as

> depreciation—a non-cash deduction
> capital gains—taxed at lower rates
> installment sales—latitude in deciding when you
>   have the profit taxed
> exchanges—the ability to get out of title to rental
>   property without paying taxes on the gain.

Couple those tax benefits with the considerations an investor is looking for in an investment such as

> leverage
> inflation protection
> liquidity
> diversification
> safety
> management

Those all come combined in the ownership of single-family homes.

Although personal experience is the best test of any investment, the fact that single-family homes are the next-best investment to owning your own home can be measured by anyone. List all the investment alternatives that may interest you, and then rate each of them on a scale of one to ten, with ten being best according to the seven benefits above (six plus tax benefits) that an investor is looking for. No matter who rates them objectively, single-family homes will come out a consistent winner.

In fact, in my judgment, good Christian stewards would not have any other kind of investment until they owned between five and ten single-family homes.

LIST OF ADVANTAGES

Study the following list of advantages carefully, keeping in mind that single-family homes must be compared against other investment alternatives.

1. *Ownership of single-family homes is understood by the average person.* Compare single-family homes with the stock market or commodities regarding the individuals ability to understand them.

2. *Single-family homes are available in large quantities throughout the country, and there is a wide range of sizes and styles available.* This is not true of art, sculpture, diamonds, and many other kinds of investments.

3. *There is a large and continued demand for single-family homes.* The American dream of owning your own home has not changed and appears unlikely to change. The ability to readily identify the goal of ownership makes a single-family home an ideal objective for the success-oriented individual.

4. *Single-family homes can be bought for under their true market value.* In many cases, the seller is under pressure to sell, and even a 10 percent discount under market price can result in a major return on cash invested.

5. *A major portion of single-family homes are owned by users.* That lends stability to the marketplace and is a deterrent to a major depression in prices such as occurred in the stock market in the 1930s.

6. *Many single-family homes are owned free and clear or have only small loans against them.* That also has a stabilizing influence on the marketplace.

7. *Single-family homes can be purchased with flexible terms.* The seller is frequently willing to carry back paper on the sale of the property under terms and conditions that are more favorable than can normally be obtained from a financial institution.

8. *Many single-family homes have existing loans at lower-than-current interest rates that can be assumed by the buyer.* A 7 percent interest rate on a first mortgage of $50,000 with a second mortgage of $25,000 at 18 percent would average out to 10.7 percent, still well below the rate for new loans on today's market.

9. *A single-family home can be liquidated within six months.* Even with adverse conditions in the money and real estate markets, it would be unusual for a properly selected and properly priced home that was efficiently marketed to be unsold longer than six months. That is a major benefit in estates and often negates the need for expensive insurance to cover possible estate taxes.

10. *Lenders are willing to lend money to borrowers using a single-family home as security.* That is because single-family homes can be readily valued and there are customary loan-to-value ratios.

11. *Income increases at a faster rate than expenses over the years.* Since a major portion of the expenses of a single-family home consists of a fixed-loan payment, normal rent raises would increase the cash flow on a property.

12. *The tenant pays down the principal balance of the loan.* Over the years, there is a substantial equity build-up on the property from the reduction of the loan.

13. *The owner can get income tax benefits.* In the early years of ownership of a single-family home, the owner normally gets the advantage of being able to deduct depreciation and negative cash flow from ordinary income.

14. *Single-family homes do not usually fall under rent control laws.* The consumer protection movement has increased the number of local ordinances on rent control which are very much to the financial disadvantage of landlords of apartment units.

15. *A single-family home's market value is not tied to rent.* For apartment units, commercial buildings, and even the stock market, the income derived from the investment is a major item in determining the value of the asset. The value of a single-family home is determined by supply and demand and, to some extent, new construction costs.

16. *Single-family homes have a wide range of potential buyers.* "All taxpayers" could be one definition of the potential buyers. All ages and income levels can benefit through ownership. Compare the potential buyers of a single-family home to those for a duplex, triplex, or fourplex. There may be only half as many or even fewer buyers for those. That may not be strictly correct, but it is true that an investor should stay in the mass market as much as possible.

17. *Single-family home purchasing does not necessarily require a large amount of cash.* If necessary, it is possible to buy a house with little or no money down. Another way of saying this is that you can buy using "other people's money." Granted, that will tend to give rise to high monthly payments, but that is no different from the way many Americans purchase their residences or pay their taxes.

18. *Single-family homes are an excellent investment to hold for a retirement portfolio.* Since single-family homes tend to appreciate in inflationary times, they are a much better investment than a money instrument for someone planning for retirement.

19. *A single-family home doubles in price in five years.* Is that an advantage? Of course it is, and yet many people overlook it. If you don't agree with the statement, put in your own figure or, better still, invest in one of the many areas where it is true.

20. *Single-family homes can be "harvested" and "replanted."* If it is true that single-family homes double in value in five years, a program can be worked out whereby in the sixth year a house is sold. Part of the proceeds can be spent and part used to replace the house that was liquidated. This provides a continual cash flow along with maintaining an up-to-date portfolio.

21. *Used single-family homes tend to be free from government and big business intervention.*

22. Many parts of the country have substantial construction lags for single-family homes. Many single-family homes provide an opportunity for the owner to improve them and more than cover the improvement costs in a future sale. Fix-up inside and out, adding square footage, renovating, remodeling, and modernizing can frequently repay their cost many times over.

23. Inflation, pushing up travel and outside entertainment costs, plus increased leisure time, will accentuate the home as the center of family activity. Alvin Toffler, in his book *The Third Wave*, carries this thought further with his idea of "electronic cottages." He visualizes that a substantial segment of the population will be able to work out of their homes using new electronic devices to conduct their businesses.

24. With a single-family home, you don't have to make as good a deal when you buy. Compare buying several single-family homes to, say, an apartment block or a commercial building. A flaw in the purchase of the latter could be disastrous, whereas the consequences of a flaw in the purchase of a single-family home are not as serious.

25. A single-family home holds its value. Many other investments go up and down, whereas a properly selected single-family home should only increase in value.

26. Banks and financial institutions don't want them back in quantity. Many people worry about what will happen in "bad" times and overlook this important fact.

27. There is a wide latitude in how a single-family home can be liquidated. This is important for tax planning and for cash flow of the owner. The owner can become a lender and can have a secured note structured for his own needs.

28. Single-family homes are tangible. You can see them, touch them, feel them—or just kick the foundation. Compare that to the case of those people who invest in a real estate investment trust based on the quality of the brochure and a salesperson's charm.

Or compare it to a Wyoming coal mine, a boxcar, a telephone call from some boilerroom operation, Equity Funding, Chrysler, Penn Central, or Franklin National Bank.

CHARACTERISTICS OF IDEAL SINGLE-FAMILY HOME FOR RENTAL

1. *The single-family home should be located in a state that has a good economy.* The Sunbelt states, for example, would be preferred over the northern states, generally speaking.

Since inflation is not like lightning, which only strikes irregularly over an area, it is not possible for the individual to fine-tune which areas' homes are going to appreciate at a higher rate than those of other areas. But if the state is selected and major chain stores have built or are about to build in an area, the investor should feel comfortable in purchasing there if the house meets the other conditions. Macy's, Sears, Safeway, and other chains spend a lot of money in selecting good locations, and you can feel safe in following the leaders. Some people also stipulate that the house should be located adjacent to a major metropolitan area, as they think urban sprawl contributes to an above-average appreciation rate.

2. *The single-family home should be in the median level of both size and price range.* The greatest number of users or buyers is always in this middle range. In addition, the ratio of rent to market value is better at the median level than that for property with a higher market value. A $90,000 house and a $135,000 house may both rent for the same $650 per month.

3. *The single-family home should have attractive financing.* A 12 percent fixed-interest rate on an assumable loan for 60 percent of the market value would be attractive. Similarly, a 7 percent first mortgage for 30 percent of the value coupled with a 14 percent loan for 60 percent of the value would also be advantageous.

The flexibility of the seller and buyer to structure terms suitable to each other's needs is one of the major advantages in single-family homes as an investment. There are many books on the subject of financing that should be studied in detail, as there is a multitude of variations the investor can use.

4. *The single-family home should be newer rather than older.* Some people regard 10 years old as the maximum desirable; others stretch that figure to 15 years. The reasoning is that the newer the house, the less is the likelihood of major repairs being needed. In addition, in 5 or 10 years, the house will still be considered "newer."

Older properties or fix-up properties are specialized areas for people who have expertise in that field. Many people buy them as a way to get started in real estate ownership, but for the taxpayer who wants the investment to counter the tax burden and rise with inflation, they are not the correct properties to own.

5. *The single-family home should be located in an area where most of the homes are owner-occupied.* That kind of area tends to be stable, with the owners maintaining and improving their homes, which also helps to increase the market value.

PROPERTY MANAGEMENT—FEAR OF UNEXPECTED AND UNCONTROLLABLE EVENTS

"I don't want those tenant calls about the blocked drains!"

"I don't have time to manage the property!"

"How do I know the tenant isn't going to wreck the place?"

The fact is that property management is a learned skill no different from that of a carpenter, painter, or bookkeeper. If you want it done properly, hire the expert.

Just as in any other profession, there are good and bad operators, so the property manager must be checked out, too. There are property managers for single family homes who will manage the property for as little as $1 a day or a percentage of the rents, with 7-10 percent being normal. Property management is a cost of doing business, just like insurance and property taxes.

Property management is not a matter of placing an ad in the paper and renting the place to the first caller. It is a complex subject requiring systematic matching and managing of both people and property, always according to the laws in force. Many people attempt to do it themselves and hope to learn by experience. What happens is that they quickly experience things they did not even want to learn! They then either hand the problem over to other amateurs or back out of the ownership of real estate entirely.

Once you, as an investor, accept the need for professional management, you can concentrate on what you do best, which is to produce earnings and leave the management to an expert. Bringing in an expert also opens new vistas for investments, because then the property does not have to be located at the end of your nose. You are not geographically bound.

Good buys, good buyers, and good property managers will dictate where the property is located, not where the investor maintains his personal residence. There are many reasons why investors cannot buy the kind of investment real estate they should in a location close to their personal residences. Living in high-cost areas such as an affluent part of an inner city; living in a community with a nondiversified economy; or living in a declining area are justifiable reasons for not owning rental property in your home town.   Learn property management on the job if you will. However, as soon as you have learned enough, hand it over to those who are better trained and qualified to do it.

CHAPTER 11

When to Sell

No Fixed Formula

"When do I sell?" Many people think there should be a fixed formula for the sale of an investment. They would like to know how many years they should hold rental property, when to take a profit in a stock, when to take a loss. Sorry, there is no formula, no rule of thumb, for when to sell. Any formula you may have encountered in the past is wrong!

However it is not quite as bleak as that. The decision to sell cannot be made on its own. Again, all the net worth figures have to be examined, and the effect a sale would have on the other investments has to be calculated.

Let us examine the "sell" problem in more detail. This book has been concerned with the "buy" problem, which is a decision people have to learn to make. The who, what, where, how, and why for the "buy" decision ought now to be understood.

Many people make the buy decision—and stop. They may even make the decision a second time—and stop. But it is just as important to know when to make the other decisions as it is to know when to make the first. Those decisions include the following:

> hold
> sell
> refinance
> exchange
> installment sale

HOLD

Let it be said again that the key to making any investment decision is the measurement of net worth on a quarterly basis and the systematic review of each item to determine if a change should be made.

It is not usually difficult to reach a "hold" decision. An investment was usually made to achieve certain objectives and benefits. When the investment is proceeding according to plan, the "hold" decision is usually the proper one to make.

SELL

The sell decision may come in two ways. It may be a forced decision because the proceeds are needed for further investment or to satisfy liquidity problems. Or it may be a decision made because the goals have been reached, the benefits obtained, and the funds could be put to use elsewhere.

The income tax implications must be investigated before any decision to sell is reached. The sale of an investment normally triggers a capital gain (or loss), and the timing of the sale becomes important. If it is made early in the year, there may be an opportunity to offset the gain by buying additional deductions. That is not the case if the sale is made in the latter months of a year.

A forced sale should be avoided wherever possible, as that tends to reduce the proceeds and provide less-beneficial terms to the seller. Liquidity has been stressed throughout, and there may be other ways to raise cash for a short time so that the sale can be made in the ordinary course of events, thus protecting the rights of the seller. Good banking relationships are so important here, and most people do not use banks often enough to prevent a forced sale. The function of a bank is to provide funds that bridge a time gap. Given adequate security and return, banks may be only too pleased to wait out the time until an advantageous sale can be consummated.

Many people continue to ignore the sell signal that was given to rental property by the 1981 Income Tax Act. Anyone who owns a piece of rental property purchased prior to 1981 and that has been held for two years or longer, *must* consider selling it. The reason is that it may be possible to sell the property, reinvest some of the proceeds, put some in your pocket, and not pay taxes on the sale.

Here is an example. A rental property was purchased several years ago that is valued as follows:

Market value	$100,000
Less loan	(25,000)
Equity	75,000

The property currently rents for more than expenses. The annual positive cash flow of $1,000 is offset by the depreciation figure of $1,000, so that the property is no longer giving the holder any tax benefits. If the property were sold, the following may result:

Market value	$100,000
Cost basis + sale expenses	(40,000)
Gain on sale	60,000
Capital gains rate 40%	24,000

In the year of sale, $24,000 would be added to the taxpayer's ordinary income. The objective, therefore, is to determine if the proceeds of $75,000 can be reinvested under the new depreciation rules and buy enough deductions to offset the gain incurred.

In today's marketplace, the seller frequently has to be responsible for a portion of the financing in order for a sale to be put together. We will assume that the $75,000 proceeds yielded $60,000 in cash for possible reinvestment and a $15,000 note.

Suppose our imaginary investor buys a rental house of double the value of the old one, purchasing on a breakeven basis. The following would be the numbers on the property purchased:

Market value	$200,000
Loans	(140,000)
Down payment	60,000
	Breakeven

Depreciation	$\dfrac{150,000}{15} = \$10,000$
Accelerated depreciation	$17,500

The accelerated depreciation figure is not enough to offset all the gain of $24,000, but it is getting close.

Suppose instead our investor buys a house with negative cash flow. The figures might now be:

Market value	$300,000
Loan	(240,000)
Down payment	60,000
	Negative

Depreciation $\dfrac{225,000}{15} = \$15,000$

Accelerated depreciation $26,250

The $26,250 more than exceeds the $24,000 gain, but at this level there is a substantial negative cash flow. However, the interest received on the $15,000 note would help to offset some of the negative cash flow.

From these calculations, it appears that serious consideration should be given to selling the property. The seller now knows what can be achieved with a sale and would structure both the sell and buy transactions to achieve the objective.

The advantages of a properly timed sell decision are substantial and would be as follows:

1. It would be possible to offset most if not all of any gain in the year of sale.

2. Income tax deductions of $10,000 and more would be available in future years, compared with zero deductions from continued ownership.

3. Three times as much value of property would be owned as before.

The next step would be to examine the effect a sale would have on the rest of the net worth statement, then call in the accountant and real estate broker to check the calculations and put together a sell-buy package.

Never Turn Residence into Rental

A common mistake made by many homeowners is to vacate

their personal residence, buy another house to live in, then convert their first house into rental property.

That is a totally wrong move for several reasons. Normally, the reasoning behind such a move is that the house can be rented for more than the loan payment; the difference between the rent and the loan payment can then be used by the owner to help make the payment on the mortgage on the new residence. The problem is that the excess rent results in more taxable income to the owner. Since that would always be taxed at the highest tax rate, possibly 50 percent of the income could be paid out in taxes.

In addition, the basis for depreciation for the rental is the original purchase price of the residence. That is frequently a low percentage of the total market value, which results in a lower depreciation deduction than could normally be anticipated. Here's an example:

Residence cost	$45,000
Current market value	100,000
Loan	(35,000)
Equity	$65,000
Loan payment	$350 per month

Residence turned into rental:

Rent	$650
Loan payment	(350)
Surplus added to income	$300 per month

Depreciation is based on $45,000 of property when $100,000 is owned. The owners are giving themselves two problems. They are adding to their taxable income $3,600 per year. And they are reducing their potential depreciation. Why depreciate $45,000 of real estate when you own $100,000?

Refinancing not a solution

Many people, being aware of that problem, attempt to correct it by refinancing the residence. The higher loan payments then offset the rental income, thus correcting the more-taxable-income problem.

That is, however, a halfway solution only. The refinancing does not change the basis for depreciation of the rental. The basis remains the original cost of the property.

Keep residential and rental tax benefits separate.

In the Internal Revenue Service code there are several benefits accorded to the owner of a personal residence—the ability to sell and buy a more expensive one and defer taxes on the sale, $125,000 one time tax free, and so on.

There are also several benefits in the Internal Revenue Service code that apply to rental property—depreciation, the ability to exchange, and so on. Those benefits are important. They are different. They must never be mixed.

Turning a residence into a rental would look like this:

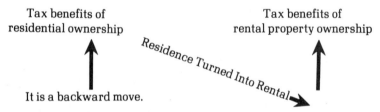

Tax benefits of residential ownership

Tax benefits of rental property ownership

Residence Turned Into Rental

It is a backward move.

If a benefit is accorded a taxpayer, it is vital that the taxpayer take the benefit. The ability to sell a residence and defer payment of taxes on the gain if the property is replaced by one more expensive is one of the most lucrative benefits a taxpayer could desire. *Always*

> sell the residence
> buy a more expensive one
> finance the new residence properly
> If there are funds left over, buy a rental property.

Never turn a residence into a rental.

REFINANCE

Refinancing is a method to change the financing on a piece of real estate. The effect is normally three-fold:

> 1. The costs of ownership are usually substantially increased because of higher interest rates.

2. Additional funds are available for the investor's use.

3. There has been a substantial change made to the investor's tax return.

The math of the transaction can be calculated reasonably precisely so that the investor is left with the classic cost-benefit question. Do the benefits received exceed the costs of implementing the transaction in this and future years?

Refinancing is not an easy decision to make, particularly since the new interest rate may be more than double the previous one. Again, it is important that this interest rate is studied in the context of the entire net worth statement. Most people would prefer paying interest rather than taxes. Taxes are definite and are money lost forever as soon as they are paid. Interest can also be considered lost; however, the property the interest is being paid on is certainly not lost and may in the long run appreciate by much more than the interest paid out.

A refinancing possibility occurs when a property has too much equity in it. What is "too much"? Since the figure varies according to a taxpayer's financial condition, a measure of "too much" should be tied to the annual earnings of the family. If a family earns $20,000 per year, they enjoy a $20,000 a year lifestyle. If they earn $40,000, it is a $40,000 a year lifestyle. Liquidity can therefore be measured in the same way. The funds to replace the first family's earnings for a full year may be around $20,000; the second would need $40,000. That is a generous method of measuring liquidity, since it would be unlikely for a family to be in a situation that continued for a full year before other sources of income could be brought into being.

Liquidity, as has been noted, is an integral part of a net worth statement. It therefore follows that a $20,000 income family should not be holding investments with more than $20,000 equity in them. The $20,000 equity represents one year's buying power to that family. A $40,000 family should strive to have a series of investments that has under $40,000 of equity in each. In hard times, they can pick and choose which one to liquidate. Conversely, if the $40,000 family had only one investment with $175,000 of equity, they might find it more difficult to sell since there are fewer potential buyers at that level and the sale would undoubtedly give rise to severe tax problems.

"Too much" equity is a frequent condition in net worth statements and is an indication that proper stewardship is not being practiced. It is surprising how many people buy and hold and go no further. The inevitable result is that they use up their tax benefits and end up with a more serious tax problem than ever.

EXCHANGE

Prior to the 1981 tax act, exchanges were a popular method of deferring taxes. With the new, liberal depreciation provisions, it may be advantageous to sell and reinvest as was illustrated before. Real estate exchanges require a certain amount of expertise to put together, but competent people with that skill can be found in all areas of the country. Call your best escrow officer for their names.

INSTALLMENT SALES

The rules regarding installment sales were amended in recent years and are now very much in favor of the taxpayer. The taxpayer has the option of deciding when the proceeds of a sale are taxed—in the year of sale or in the taxable years the proceeds are received.

This installment sale option is a very useful tool for taxpayers and is a further reason that a sale *must* be discussed with the tax adviser before any papers are drawn.

The following shows how an installment sale can be structured to spread the gain over three tax years but deliver the proceeds in thirteen months:

First installment December 15—tax year 1
Second installment January 15—tax year 2
Third installment January 15—tax year 3

CHAPTER 12

Will

PROTECTION OF NET WORTH

This book has been concerned with good Christian stewardship regarding the accumulation of net worth. Good stewardship also requires the protection of net worth. You have to have a will. As soon as you become a taxpayer, you should have a properly drawn up, legally prepared will. A written or holographic will, or a will filled out on a mass-produced form from a stationery store, makes no sense at all at any level of an estate.

If you do not have a will, the state will write one for you according to the law—not the needs, wants, and desires of the participants. Yet strange as it may seem, it is said that over 70 percent of taxpayers do not have a will.

Do you even know what the laws regarding inheritance are in your state? What happens if you have adopted children, step-children, errant children, aged parents, needy relatives, or strong religious convictions? Will any of the money go to churches, missionaries, and other Christian works and workers you have supported in life? Is it wise to allow the state to decide how the funds should be distributed? The value of the estate will also be reduced by expensive attorneys' fees. It is not good stewardship at all to accumulate net worth if you are not going to protect it.

Once a will is prepared, it should be reviewed at least once every three years and amended as necessary to take care of changing circumstances.

ESTATE TAXES

The estate of a deceased, as distinct from the net worth described in this book, includes all the furniture and personal effects of the deceased, so the estate will be higher than the net worth.

At a certain level of estate, estate or inheritance taxes come into play. The estate tax rates are every bit as onerous as income tax, and again, there is no excuse for paying them. The 1981 tax act saw major changes in estate taxes, so much so that anyone who prepared a will prior to 1981 should immediately review it with an attorney. One change concerned the value at which an estate became liable to pay estate taxes. The figure for many years had been approximately $175,000 and had been outdated because of inflation. That figure is being phased upward until it reaches $600,000 in 1987.

Other important changes concerned the ability of a surviving spouse to inherit the deceased's estate tax-free, with the result that a properly drawn will, using a marital trust, may be able to pass on to heirs a $1.2 million estate tax-free.

Owners of estates that are now valued substantially higher than the $175,000 figure mentioned should take specific action to protect against estate taxes. That generally requires the setting up of trusts. The services and advice of a good estate tax attorney are necessary. The best method of selecting this expert is by reference from friends and relatives who may have had similar problems.

Every taxpayer should have a will and the next of kin should be notified of three things:

1. There is a will.
2. Where the will is located.
3. Who has been selected to administer the will.

CHAPTER 13

Solutions to Personal Money Management Problems

Chapter 4 identified the items on a net worth statement that would precipitate corrective action being taken. Now that the subject of personal money management has been examined in detail, the solution to each of those problems should be studied by the reader.

These solutions are listed below in the same sequence as the problems were identified in chapter 4, and changes should be made if any of the following is true:

1. Personal residence needs to be changed.

The existing residence is not the most suitable place for the family to be living in for the next three years. The residence should be the right size, shape, and location for the needs, wants, and desires of the family, with prudent limitations.

Solution. Sell the residence, taking advantage of the rules regarding deferment of taxes on any gain on a sale, and purchase a more suitable residence.

2. Equity in personal residence is too high.

There is too much equity in the personal residence, and taxes paid are high.

Solution. There are two alternatives. (1) Release the equity by selling the house and buying another one that has different financing. (2) Release the equity by changing the financing. Either rewrite the first mortgage or take out a second mortgage. The additional interest payments will reduce the taxable income.

3. The personal residence has more than one mortgage against it.

Generally speaking, there is financial security in having only a first mortgage against the personal residence. The reason is that if there is ever a cash shortage, you can always get a second loan using the house as security.

Solution. Since the personal residence is the best investment a family owns, it should have secure, long-term financing against it. Either a new first mortgage should be taken out, consolidating all other loans, or the property should be sold and a replacement purchased that is properly financed.

4. The personal residence has a loan against it that has a short-term balloon payment due, and you probably won't be able to pay it.

Since the personal residence is the best investment a family owns, it should have secure, long-term financing against it.

Solution. The residence should be refinanced.

5. A rental property has excess equity, and taxes paid are high.

The equity can be used to purchase tax deductions to reduce the tax bill.

Solution. The equity should be released and put to work buying additional property that will help reduce the tax bill.

6. A rental property has positive cash flow, and taxes paid are high.

The positive cash flow is compounding the tax problem.

Solution. The property may have outlived its usefulness and may have to be sold or exchanged, or at least refinanced, to cure the positive cash flow problem.

7. There is insurance cash value and a substantial net worth.

There comes a time when the need for insurance ceases because the net worth has risen high enough.

Solution. The money used to pay premiums should be switched to a better investment vehicle. The insurance can remain in force if necessary, with the premiums being paid from the cash value.

8. There is no pension plan.

A pension contribution is an easy and beneficial income tax deduction, and there would have to be a good reason why it was not taken.

Solution. A pension plan is a systematic savings program that compounds without tax consequences. It would be most unusual for a taxpayer under 65 not to have a pension plan.

9. There is excess savings.

We will examine later why any savings may be excessive. Savings is an underutilization of funds and must be kept to a minimum. Savings yield interest, which is a taxable surplus (above a small minimum) and should be avoided.

Solution. The savings should be reinvested in an asset that is subjected to inflation. Savings yields interest, and most interest is taxable. All surplus taxable income should be avoided.

10. There are stock investments, and taxes are being paid.

Since stocks can be owned by a pension plan that does not

have tax consequences when stocks are bought and sold, it would be unusual for an individual to own stocks in his own name.

Solution. The stocks should be sold and the proceeds invested in an asset that provides income tax deductions.

11. The net worth is under $1 million and the leverage ratio is low.

In an inflationary economy, you are not going to make money unless you borrow money.

If you want to be a millionaire, acquire $1 million of assets, whether they are paid for or not.

Solution. There is a need to strive for financial security (which is being identified as $1 million of net worth), so the borrowings have to be increased, which will in turn increase the leverage ratio.

12. The gross earnings are low.

Yes, this is a problem! Perhaps some family members are not using their time and talents to optimum capacity. Earnings have to be sufficient to cover tithing, subsistence, and a provision for the future.

Solution. Reexamine the goals and objectives of each family member, and take the training or get the experience necessary to increase the gross earnings.

13. Income taxes paid are high.

Over $10,000 a year is high!
Over $5,000 a year is high!
Much less is acceptable!
Between zero and $4-5,000 a year is permissible.

Solution. Get more income tax deductions.

14. There is material capital gain in an asset.

A major capital gain can be a ticking time bomb, and the asset may need to be broken down into smaller assets.

Solution. Income tax deductions must be secured that will offset the capital gain. Frequently these can only be obtained by the sale of the asset itself, so it is essential that the sale is tax-planned months or even years in advance.

15. *Notes receivable are high, and income tax paid is high.*

The notes yield interest that is compounding the tax problem.

Solution. Reduce the notes receivable either by discounting them or using them as a down payment on an asset that yields income tax deductions.

16. *There is too much equity in any one asset.*

"Too much" could be defined as equity in excess of one year's earnings. This can cause a liquidity problem.

Solution. Release the equity, probably by a sale, before it causes a major liquidity or capital gains problem.

17. *Only purchases have been made.*

Buying is one decision. It is equally important to know when to sell, refinance, or exchange. Assets outlive their usefulness, and benefits get used up.

Solution. The proper move will have been covered in one of the other solutions.

18. *Taxpayers do not own a single-family home.*

Since they are taxpayers, they are not using one of the best income tax deductions available, the benefits of property ownership.
They do not necessarily have to live in the home; they can use it as rental property.

Solution. Buy one! Buy one to fit the financial circumstances of the taxpayer and in a state with an expanding economy.

19. There are not enough assets riding with inflation.

Single-family homes do, treasury bills do not.

Solution. Never get totally out of the inflationary spiral. Never retire from investing—only God knows how long you are going to live. Always own some improved real estate.

20. There is limited or no diversification or liquidity.

All net worth statements must contain diversification and liquidity.

Solution. Diversify! Get liquid! Get negative savings. Always be ready, be prepared. We do not know what is going to happen in the future, so the only prudent thing is to diversify.

21. There are assets with no known value.

People may have moved out of state and still own land, or they may have inherited property many miles away. Or they may even have substantial family silver or jewelry in their own vault. It is not uncommon for people to overlook valuable assets.

Solution. List *all* assets on a quarterly basis, and have those with no readily determinable value appraised at least every three-five years.

22. Wrong assets are held.

Bare land (builders and developers make the profit here), commercial buildings, inherited stocks—there are many examples of wrong assets to be found in any given individual portfolio.

Solution. Liquidate the assets and reinvest the proceeds in an asset that will improve the portfolio.

SINGLE FAMILY HOME RENTAL PROPERTY EXAMPLE

This is a profile of a single family home rental property but we must realize it can be dangerous to produce numbers like these — there is no typical property, the same as there is no typical citizen. Those who have no investment experience whatsoever can use the numbers as a guide in what to expect from single family home investment.

Each one of the lines shown can vary by substantial margins which in turn causes substantial repercussions in the other calculations. For example, putting less or more money down will affect the monthly outflow, tax benefits and return on investment.

Buy an investment like one of these shown though, and it will surely and steadily work for you over the months and years. The monthly outflow will reduce as rents increase, and equity in the property will increase as inflation marches along.

Purchase price	$95,000
Assume existing loans	68,000
New loans	8,000
Down payment	19,000
Monthly rent	500
Principal, interest, taxes	
insurance, repairs, management	850
Additional monthly investment	350
Tax deduction, first year	4,200
Depreciation	
purchase price less 20% for land—	
straight line 15 years	5,067
Total tax deductions	9,267
Cash invested first year	$23,200
Estimated return	
10% appreciation	9,500
50% tax bracket	4,638
	$14,138
Return on investment	61%

CHAPTER 14

Case Studies

PIECING THE PUZZLE TOGETHER

The pieces of the puzzle have been described. How do all of them fit together so that a Christian is secure in the knowledge that he is practicing sound personal money management and good stewardship?

Some case studies are presented that illustrate many of the points made and principles outlined. Your own personal situation is unique, and although numerical solutions can be found for any given situation, that is only half the answer. Those numerical solutions then have to be applied to the expertise, desires, wants, preferences, and all the other items that go to make up the individual. That is where the fee-based financial consultant is used.

However, now that we are equipped with the knowledge of the principles involved, and with our continuing source of guidance and strength from above sought in prayer, we, too, can become good Christian stewards.

The case studies have been arranged in ascending order of complexity. Each case study has been based on factual situations in California, and the numbers can be scaled up or down to fit the numbers in other states.

Not all the facts of each case have been recorded—only those important to the points discussed. It would normally be

117

found that there are several financial moves that have to be made, and also several alternatives to a problem. When the moves are known, the one having the greatest financial impact should be selected. That would be done first and would be accorded top priority. Future quarterly reviews of the net worth statement will bring out different moves and priorities whenever conditions change.

Case Study 1   Pre-investment years

Assets	Zero
Earnings	$30,000
Age	30

At a young age, the attention should be focused on stabilizing a career and raising the earnings. Therefore, prior to age 30 it is not necessary to become involved in serious net worth accumulation. During this period a person may dabble with and gain experience in such vehicles as savings accounts, renting, possibly the stock market and life insurance, but major investments are not critical. The emphasis should be on developing the career even though the amount of taxes paid becomes substantial.

Frequently parents despair that their children are not being "responsible" because their early career paychecks go toward capital items and "frivolous" purchases. This is all part of life's learning experience and it is better to get it out of the way before a person settles down to providing for a family.

But pass 30, or exceed $30,000 in earnings, and you MUST START on a planned net worth accumulation program. And this age of 30 could be reduced somewhat if a couple marries at a young age and begins to raise a family.

Case Study 2   Starter

Couple, early 30s
No dependents

Land	$5,000
Savings	5,000
Automobiles	12,000
Auto loan	(2,000)
Insurance cash value	2,000
Total assets	$24,000
Total liabilities	(2,000)
Net worth	$22,000
Leverage	8%
Gross earnings	$30,000
Taxes	8,000

It is not too difficult to see that this couple should try to buy a personal residence and use the advantage of leverage to reduce the tax burden.

However, there is some genuine resistance. They have made two prior investments that did not work out, one in land, the other in insurance. Both of those investments are the wrong ones for this couple.

Solution: There is a real need for them to get started practicing good Christian stewardship. They have to purchase their own residence.

The down payment can be raised in a wide variety of ways:
sale of existing assets—land
government financing programs for owner-
    occupier
friends, relatives, employer
savings, credit union, credit cards, credit line
sale or pledge of personal property—auto
cash value of insurance

They must beg, borrow, scrape, save, negotiate, and whatever else is necessary to get title to that first piece of real estate.

Case Study 3   Slow Mover

House	$80,000
Loan	(20,000)
	60,000
Earnings	$45,000

This is the typical case of a taxpayer who has bought a personal residence and has stayed there too long.

The income level has increased steadily over the years but the taxpayer has not continued to take advantage of the two major income tax benefits accorded to homeowners—the ability to sell and purchase a more expensive residence without paying taxes on the sale, and the ability to deduct a substantial house payment.

Financial institutions have various guidelines as to how much an individual may borrow. These guidelines for most homeowners are based upon their income level. If the guideline is 2 to 3 times the annual gross income, this means that this taxpayer could have a loan of about $100,000.

In financial planning and personal money management, the converse is also true. If a financial institution is willing to lend $100,000 and an individual has only borrowed $20,000, then there are underutilized funds with which to start an investment program even if part of these funds are set aside to make payments.

Solution: In this case, the taxpayer should buy a more expensive residence since one's house is the single best investment. With the funds left over he could embark on an investment program in single family homes.

It would not be unusual to end up with $250,000 to $350,000 of real estate including a new personal residence. The corresponding income tax benefits plus the greatly increased stake in an asset which will increase in value in the inflationary spiral will start him on the road to financial security.

Case Study 4	Buy and hold
Residence	$150,000
Loan	(25,000)
Rental house	75,000
Loan	(20,000)
Rental house	55,000
Loan	(20,000)
Rental house	60,000
Loan	(15,000)
Cash	15,000
Total assets	$355,000
Total liabilities	(80,000)
Net worth	$275,000
Earnings	$50,000

This couple has done well. They are on the way to accumulating a sizable net worth with the consistent acquisition of single family homes. However, that is all they have done. It is just as important to know when to sell, exchange or refinance as it is to know when to buy.

Their problem is that they are paying one third of their income in taxes. The properties have all passed the point of benefiting the taxpayer and are adding to the tax problem by producing positive cash flow. Sure, it is nice to own attractive properties, lots of equity, positive cash flow—but not if it's going to cost $18,000 a year in taxes!

In this case the taxpayer can afford to keep the larger equity in the personal residence because they are already along the path of building a good net worth. This equity is also a means of security, providing substantial borrowing power in case a reversal of fortunes should occur.

Solution: Since the investment properties have probably been held for a long time and have a low basis, a sale or refinance program should be scheduled over the next few years and the proceeds combined with the savings, and reinvested in additional single family homes.

Case Study 5   Property held 3 + years

		IRS
Rental	$100,000	Net sales price
Loan	(40,000)	Basis
Equity	$60,000	Long term capital gain

Play the rules of the game as they are today! If they change the rules, you must change your game plan.

The Economic Recovery Tax Act of 1981 produced many significant changes of great importance to all taxpayers. It again emphasizes the importance of measuring your net worth on a quarterly basis and adjusting to suit the times.

As an example, we shall check to see how the act makes it necessary for a taxpayer to consider selling any property held longer than three years. The proceeds should be reinvested and no taxes paid on the sale! The example illustrates the material advantage the taxpayer has under the new depreciation rules as compared to the old depreciation rules.

The three years quoted is the author's figure and represents a timespan where there has been sufficient appreciation in the property to make the exercise worthwhile.

For ease of explanation the same figures have been used for both the taxpayer and the Internal Revenue Service.

The property appeared on the taxpayer's return for last year. Readers familiar with rental property will agree that the values shown indicate the property was held on a break-even basis. In other words the rental income was totally offset by the expenses of holding the property—principal, interest, taxes, insurance, vacancy, repairs and management. This also indicates that the cash transactions from the property did not affect the taxable income.

The taxpayer had been claiming depreciation according to the rules in force so let us assume the depreciation was $1,000 per year.

In other words the taxpayer enjoyed $1,000 as a deduction on last year's tax return.

Let us examine the effects of a sale and a reinvestment of the proceeds. We will look at a straightforward sale first and later check on some variables which the marketplace may dictate.

A sale may produce $60,000 cash for the taxpayer, but would

also result in $60,000 of long term capital gain. Of this gain, 40 percent, or $24,000, would be added to the taxpayer's other income in the year of sale. This could greatly increase the taxes paid unless further action was taken to offset this.

Let us say the taxpayer follows the principles in this book and reinvests the proceeds of $60,000 in single family homes— possibly four rental properties are purchased and existing financing taken over from the sellers.

Properties purchased	$240,000
Loans	(180,000)
Down payment	$ 60,000

The property purchased can be depreciated under the new depreciation rules. There are two alternatives: either the building can be written off over 15 years straight line, or the accelerated rate which is 175% of the straight line can be used in the first year. The calculation may be

Land	$ 60,000
Building	180,000
Property purchased	$240,000
Depreciation	$180,000 ÷ 15 = $12,000 straight line or
	175% of $12,000 = $21,000 accelerated

In addition let's assume that the four houses did not generate enough rental income to cover all of the expenses of holding the property. In fact each house required $150 per month to support it.

This negative cash flow is also an income tax deduction so four houses would produce a deduction of 4 × $150 per month × 12 months = $7,200 per year.

In other words it may be possible to generate $28,200 of deductions ($21,000 depreciation plus $7,200 negative cash flow) to more than offset the $24,000 of capital gains!

That is the example in its simplest form. It is a demonstration of how the new depreciation rules are so much more beneficial than the old ones and it may be possible to change properties without major tax consequences.

However certain other variables have to be considered before the taxpayer decides to make the move.

Factors operating against the taxpayer

1. It would be unlikely that the property would realize $60,000 cash in today's marketplace. It would be realistic to assume that the buyer made a small cash downpayment and had the seller carry a substantial note secured by the property. This is not necessarily a deterrent to the sale. It may be possible to discount the note substantially and still have the numbers operate in favor of the taxpayer.

2. The taxpayer may not be able to support the negative cash flow shown. It is important that an example like this be considered in the context of the entire net worth of the taxpayer. But it would be most likely—when all factors are considered—that the taxpayer would decide to proceed with at least a modified version of the transaction.

3. The tax deductions illustrated have been calculated for a full year whereas they would be prorated according to when the transaction took place during the year.

4. The sale could result in a minimal tax becoming due under the tax preference rules.

Factors operating in favor of the taxpayer

1. The ability to abandon a $1,000 deduction from the old property and convert that into a deduction materially greater (up to $28,200 in the example) presents an overwhelming reason to come up with some acceptable transaction.

2. The ability to take a large profit ($60,000) and reinvest it in several more assets (four) and yet only pay a few thousand dollars in taxes is another major incentive to come up with a workable solution.

3. The installment sale rules whereby a taxpayer can time the receipt of the cash and the tax consequences over different tax years could well offset the problem incurred by having to prorate the deductions.

Solution: If a taxpayer has held a piece of property longer than three years selling it and reinvesting the proceeds must be considered. The taxpayer's financial consultant or real estate agent, in conjunction with the tax preparer, can calculate various mathematical models which will probably show that a sell decision would be dramatically more beneficial to the taxpayer than a hold decision.

Case Study 6   Mother-in-law's munificence

Son
Residence	$150,000
Loan	(50,000)
Net worth	$100,000
Gross earnings	$ 75,000

Mother-in-law
Residence	$150,000
Money instruments	250,000
Net worth	$400,000
Retired	

This is a classic case of the family having to unite to save with those two institutions, the Internal Revenue Service and the lenders.

Both families are paying substantial amounts of income tax, and the only apparent deduction is about $5,000 of interest from the house mortgage.

The mother-in-law has more than enough income to meet her immediate needs, but her estate is dwindling as the purchasing power of the dollar decreases. She is no longer using the principle of leverage to maintain or increase her net worth.

Solution: The son should take advantage of being able to move into a more expensive house and raise his interest deduction for income tax.

The mother-in-law would be well-advised to leave only $50,000 tied up in money instruments. With no house payments, she could live off interest and capital for a few years before that is totally depleted.

The $200,000 remaining should be invested in single-family homes. The mother-in-law may buy two in her name to shelter her income and then lend the balance to her son to buy in his name. As security for the note, she would take a blanket lien against all the property purchased by the son, including his residence, if desired.

If the son purchased aggressively with advantageous terms from the seller and left some of the proceeds in a fund to cover negative cash flows for a couple of years, his income tax bill would be greatly reduced.

One further advantage is that the son would learn how to invest while his mother-in-law was alive. It is totally wrong (and yet it is frequently done) for a substantial inheritance to be dumped on people who have had no training or experience in handling money.

If the older parent needs additional funds in the future, more of the properties can be sold off under terms sufficient to meet the income needs.

The 4-5 single-family homes purchased, plus the increased house payment, would result in a reduction of $15,000 or more in the income tax bill.

Case Study 7   Family united

Mother
Income: Social Security
2 married sons

House	$100,000
Loan	(15,000)
Net worth	$ 85,000

The corollary to the previous example brings a similar solution. The parent may be on a small, fixed income and yet have considerable equity tied up in the house. A fixed income in inflationary times is the most difficult financial condition of all. The standard of living is gradually eroded over the years until the individual is merely existing. The addition of even a few hundred dollars a month represents untold riches in cases such as those.

It may be that the parent has sons or daughters. Investigation may find that they are now married, raising families, owning their own homes. Both spouses are working. Such a scenario also means they are substantial taxpayers.

This becomes a clear case of the assets being held by the wrong party. The mother owns income tax deductions she doesn't need and has the cash locked up in equity she desperately needs.

Her family needs a rental property for investment and tax shelter. They do not want the risk of ownership and cannot afford the time to manage it, so they also would like a secure tenant.

The mother needs the security of her own place to stay and a fixed housing cost.

Solution: The solution is for the family to buy a house and rent it to the mother. The lease should be for a lifetime tenancy, and the entire contract should be designed to provide that it continues even in the case of instability of any party.

The mother sells her existing house and uses the $125,000 one-time, tax-free benefit available to those 55 or older.

She may carry back a small mortgage on the sale of this house, which supplements her monthly income. The balance of the proceeds is then reinvested in single-family homes, either in her name or in the names of the family. She accomplishes this, as in the first example, by lending them the money and taking back property as security.

Each member of the family ends up stronger. The children pay much less in taxes and have a major stake in the inflationary spiral.

It must be remembered that if nothing is done and the mother runs out of cash, she probably will end up as a dependent of her family. Few families can afford this constant drain on their resources.

In the example shown, the needs of all in the family are determined, the resources are pooled, and each one profits considerably.

Case Study 8   Wrong investments

Couple, mid 30s	
No children	
Residence	$ 80,000
Loan	(25,000)
Land in Colorado	10,000
Savings	20,000
Automobiles	10,000
Note of 10 percent due in five years	35,000
($350 per month)	
Total assets	$155,000
Total liabilities	(25,000)
Net worth	$130,000
Leverage	16%
Gross earnings	$25,000

This couple are approaching their peak earning years. The first item to be examined would be their gross earnings to make certain they were using their time and talents to the greatest advantage. If not, increasing the earnings might become the top priority.

Assuming that the earnings are in line, this couple are not sufficiently leveraged and are in the wrong investments. They have moved about the country and left relics of investments behind. When they lived in Colorado twelve years ago, they put a down payment on a piece of land that has now doubled in price. Sorry, that's not a good investment to only have doubled in the last twelve years. Their market value estimate could be off by as much as 50 percent ($8-12,000) if they have not kept up with prices there.

(Note: Items such as the Colorado land are frequently found in portfolios and dismissed by the owners as not important. That is not so. Ten thousand dollars is a handsome sum. In addition, as years go by the owners tend to drift further and further away from their original goals in making the purchase.)

A five year note is also a totally wrong investment for this couple. Interest from this, plus savings interest, is raising their tax bill considerably. A couple in their mid 30s should not need the regular cash flow a note payment provides—retired people, on the other hand, do need it.

Solution: Check that the earnings are close to optimum.

Check that the residence is the most suitable.

Sell the Colorado land.

Take the savings and the note (discounted if necessary) and invest in single-family homes.

Case Study 9   Higher income professional

Married	
Four children	
Residence	$100,000
Loan	(25,000)
Land	125,000
Loan	(25,000)
Land partnership	50,000
Keogh—mutual fund	30,000
Autos	15,000
Bank loan	(10,000)
Total assets	$320,000
Total liabilities	(60,000)
Net worth	$260,000
Leverage	19%
Gross earnings	$ 65,000

At first glance this couple appear to be comfortably well off —worth a quarter of a million dollars and earning $65,000 a year. They invested in real estate as everyone recommended, took the pension benefits they were entitled to, and even have four children as income tax deductions. The only minor flaws seem to be that they are short of cash since they *owe* the bank $10,000 on an unsecured line of credit, and that their leverage ratio is low at 19 percent.

But wait, there is a figure missing—*all* the numbers have to be considered before a conclusion is reached. What do they pay in taxes? Twenty thousand dollars! This family is in a serious financial predicament. As the children get older, they get more expensive. Earnings have leveled off and inflation is rampant— and there is a massive tax bill.

They bought the wrong real estate, land with no tax benefits.

Solution: Sell the land (timing the sale and the conditions to minimize income tax), pay off the short-term loan to the bank, and invest the proceeds in single-family homes to yield tax deductions.

Case Study 10   Professional's problem

Age: 45-60	
Residence	$300,000
Office building—partnership	300,000
Business practice	150,000
	$750,000
Pension, gold, Tahoe lot	250,000
	$1,000,000
Earnings	$60-$75,000

Wealthy—but poor! Doctor, dentist, architect, attorney, photographer, grocer, and all those other independent business people work so hard, build a comfortable net worth—and yet, what do they have?

What would happen if the breadwinner died tomorrow? What would the surviving spouse get? Sure, a free and clear house to live in, but what else? She cannot get access to her husband's portion of the office building, the practice is no longer worth the money because the good will passed away with the owner, and little of the remaining assets are liquid.

Forced sales and inheritance taxes will slash the values of this estate even further.

All because the wrong investments are held.

All because the eggs are in one basket. There is no diversification. Granted, the office building was probably a good investment, but it has long outlived its usefulness. Each of the partners is probably paying through the nose in income taxes, both in their personal account and through their corporation if there is one.

It is normally a bad move for taxpayers to own their own office buildings or places of business. They are going totally against the principles of liquidity and diversification.

Solution: Disband the partnership on the office building and take title as tenants in common. The building can then be exchanged for whatever assets or properties each partner deems best.

If each of the partners had amassed a collection of single family homes over the years instead of the partnership building, they would not only have reduced their taxes by having to rent office space, they would have given themselves that vital ingredient of liquidity.

Note that the age of the professional is not a factor. The younger ones cannot add to their investments because their capital is locked up in the office building, and the older ones cannot retire for the same reason!

Case Study 11   Secure too soon

Couple, mid 50s	
No dependents	
Residence	$100,000
Loan	0
Rental house (cost $30,000)	75,000
Loan	(25,000)
Savings	25,000
Stocks	25,000
Total assets	$225,000
Total liabilities	(25,000)
Net worth	200,000
Leverage	11%
Gross earnings	$ 35,000

This net worth statement looks good, like the American dream, a free and clear house. However, it is too secure, too soon. This couple can reasonably anticipate living for another twenty and more years, and what are economic conditions going to be then? They must build their net worth now, while their earnings and health are good.

Their tax return shows all the wrong things. To their earnings are added three items that should be scrupulously avoided: income from the rental house, savings interest, and stock gains and dividends.

And not appearing on their tax return are some readily attainable deductions: mortgage interest on personal residence, IRA contribution, and 15-year depreciation.

(Note: The rental house will be depreciated under the pre-1981 rules, which were much less advantageous.)

The residence has to be examined in light of their needs, wants, and desires. If they intend to stay on and retire there, the luxury of having it free and clear may be justified. If, on the other hand, they intend to sell it at any time in the future, the best first mortgage should be obtained and secured against the residence. Having a good, assumable loan on the house may be an attractive feature to a future potential buyer.

Solution: Open an IRA

Sell the rental house and stocks.

Use the proceeds plus the savings to purchase single-family homes.

Case Study 12   Budget

Single, 45	
Savings	$ 5,000
Bank loan	(5,000)
Automobile	4,000
Total assets	$ 9,000
Total liabilities	(5,000)
Net worth	$ 4,000
Gross earnings	$23,000
Taxes	7,000

Here is a real inflation victim. She is self-employed and works hard to produce the income. She has never been married and does not want to change from the city lifestyle. There are no relatives or other available sources of borrowing money for a down payment, and, of course, the income level is not high enough to support substantial debt.

At the age of 45, there has got to be some concern about what will happen in older age. There is no potential of inheritance, and there are no alternative job skills that can be translated into higher income.

Solution: Marriage is one solution, but it is equally important to produce an alternative solution, quite obviously.

The other solution is the one our parents knew well and the starting point in all the older textbooks—personal budgeting and saving. For most people, it is not necessary today. If they live off their paychecks and manage their money properly, leverage and inflation will do the saving for them. After all, a portion of every mortgage payment is a reduction in principal. That is a forced saving, however small.

However, here we have a case where the only solution, however difficult, is personal savings. The best booklet to read on this topic is *The Richest Man in Babylon,* by George S. Clason. His classic line is "A part of all you earn is yours to keep."

Personal budgeting is not necessary for a lot of people, since they have considerable earning ability. It is much better to concentrate on increasing the earnings than on living frugally and saving a mite. However, the woman in this example is probably at her peak earning potential, and in this case a savings and compounding program is her only solution.

CHAPTER 15

Are You Winning?

NET WORTH GROWTH

The principles of personal money management outlined in this book work, as many satisfied clients confirm. You can believe its contents, take action, and be prosperous in the sight of the Lord and your fellow human beings, or you can quibble, delay, and do nothing.

Fortunately, financial improvement can be measured in numbers, unlike personal or spiritual growth. Measure your net worth quarterly. If your net worth at the end of the year is greater than 15 percent of the assets at the beginning of that year, you are on the right track. If not, you can anticipate finding an inability to maintain your accustomed standard of living in the inflationary years ahead. This drop could be so severe that you might go all the way back to where you started—with nothing, and dependent on others for support. (Fifteen percent is used because, we hope, this is ahead of the rate of inflation.)

Here is the calculation with some sample figures:

	December	March	June	September	December
Assets	100,000				150,000
Liabilities	(60,000)				(90,000)
Net worth	40,000				60,000
Assets at beginning of year					100,000
15 percent targeted gain					15,000
Net worth at start of year					40,000
Targeted net worth at end of year					55,000
Actual net worth					60,000
Ahead of target					5,000

Failure to achieve targeted growth indicates that there is a flaw in the net worth business. The five business components described earlier—purchasing, production, administration, marketing, and selling—have to be reexamined to make sure they are all functioning adequately.

BUILD ON A FIRM FOUNDATION

Here is the sequence for successful Christian stewardship:

1. *Devotion to God.* "Seek ye first the kingdom of God, and his righteousness; and all these things shall be added unto you" (Matt. 6:33). Total allegiance to God and devotion to serving His cause are essential to any true success. Daily prayer and time in the Bible will provide the guidance necessary to embark on the next steps.

Remember, too, that there can be no real success in any area of life if you are not first in right relationship with God. "For what shall it profit a man, if he shall gain the whole world, and lose his own soul?" (Mark 8:36). "Whether therefore ye eat, or drink, or whatsoever ye do, do all to the glory of God" (1 Cor. 9:31).

2. *Family.* A solid and united family continually moving forward to predetermined goals is a vital necessity in good Christian stewardship.

3. *Earnings.* The continued development and growth of the chosen career is the next step. Note that this must not be static.

You cannot afford to be in a rut. Unless there is continual growth, the employer or the career may have to be changed.

"If any provide not for his own, and specially for those of his own house, he has denied the faith, and is worse than an infidel" (1 Tim. 5:8).

At this stage, too, the team of professional advisers will be identified, and credit lines and credit cards will be established.

No further steps will work satisfactorily if they are not launched from a stable earning base.

4. *Residence.* Development of the net worth business occurs after stable earnings have been achieved, and the first move is normally ownership of the personal residence. The residence should be continually changed and upgraded, helping the owner to counter inflation and take advantage of income tax benefits.

5. *Reduce taxes.* A concentrated effort has to be made to become aware of the tax laws and take advantage of them. Education, record-keeping, and a plan to take advantage of all available deductions is the next link in the chain.

6. *Develop investments.* Ownership of single family homes will probably take place concurrently with the investing of the pension plan, probably in the stock market or money market funds.

Liquidity and diversification will be constantly monitored, and the net worth statement will be measured quarterly.

Traveling safely through those six steps will bring the sweetest-sounding words to the ears of the Christian steward:

> Well done, thou good and faithful servant: thou hast been faithful over a few things, I will make thee ruler over many things: enter thou into the joy of thy lord (Matt. 25:21).

CHECK LIST: WHEN DO I NEED A FINANCIAL CONSULTANT

Test yourself on the following—   YES   NO

1. Did you get an income tax refund for the last tax
    return filed?   ☐   ☐
2. Have you more than $5,000 invested in an
    interest-bearing investment—money market funds,
    treasury bills, etc.?   ☐   ☐
3. Is your current house payment under $500
    per month?   ☐   ☐
4. Do you expect to pay taxes this year?   ☐   ☐

    *Answer YES to any of the above and you need the
    services of a Financial Consultant.*

5. Do you prepare your net worth quarterly?   ☐   ☐

6. Do you have a Sears credit card?   ☐   ☐
7. Do you have an American Express card?   ☐   ☐
8. Do you have an account at a major bank?   ☐   ☐
9. Do you think inflation will continue?   ☐   ☐
10. Are you operating under a written plan for your
    net worth management this year?   ☐   ☐

11. Is your earnings goal over $50,000 this year?   ☐   ☐
12. Do you own more than five single family homes?   ☐   ☐
13. Are you a participant in a pension plan?   ☐   ☐
14. Have you changed *residences* three times in the last
    ten years?   ☐   ☐
15. Are your total liabilities greater than ⅓ of your
    total assets?   ☐   ☐

16. Does your charitable contribution claim on last year's
    tax return exceed $750?   ☐   ☐
17. Was last year's total tax bill under $5,000?   ☐   ☐
18. Do you think you have income taxes under control?   ☐   ☐
19. Have you read *Think & Grow Rich* by Napoleon Hill?   ☐   ☐
20. Have you read *How I turned $1,000 into $3,000,000
    in my spare time* by William Nickerson?   ☐   ☐

21. Do you read the *Wall Street Journal*?   ☐   ☐
22. Do you believe in capitalism?   ☐   ☐
23.. Have you reviewed your will since
    August, 1981?   ☐   ☐
24. Do you have more than $5,000 of either gold, or silver
    coins, or investment gems (do not count jewelry)?   ☐   ☐

25.	Have all members of your household closed all savings accounts earning under 8%?	☐ ☐
26.	Can you turn $20,000 of your credit into cash tomorrow?	☐ ☐
27.	Did you write more than three offers to buy property for your own account last year?	☐ ☐
28.	Do you expect and plan to be a millionaire?	☐ ☐
29.	Do you rigidly maintain separate checking accounts for personal/household items and business and/or investment items?	☐ ☐
30.	Is it usually wrong to turn a residence into a rental?	☐ ☐
31.	Is it a bad move for taxpayers to own their own office buildings?	☐ ☐
32.	Have you attended a social event in the last 12 months with— your bank manager?	☐ ☐
33.	Have you attended a social event in the last 12 months with—your tax preparer?	☐ ☐
34.	Have you/your spouse four or more Visa and Mastercharge cards?	☐ ☐
35.	Is your recordkeeping system watertight so that *all* payments for tax deductions are recorded—including cash items?	☐ ☐
36.	Are your life insurance premium payments under $500 per year?	☐ ☐
37.	Did you draft last year's income tax return prior to Dec. 31?	☐ ☐

Count the number of No's to questions 5 thru 37

0-10 No's—You're doing a pretty good job of keeping on top of your personal money management.

10-20 No's—You need help! Call in a financial consultant.

20 + No's—You're on a collision course with financial disaster. Immediate correction is required unless poverty is your goal.

EPILOGUE

By Chad Patterson Willey

I am fifteen years of age and attend Robert Louis Stevenson School in Pebble Beach, California.

I believe in God and go to Church every Sunday. I also believe in what my dad says about hard work and thrift, and I already have several investments.

I have had a bank savings account since I was very young. I deposit any cash I receive from presents for my birthday or at Christmas. When saving interest rates went to 16% (for accounts with a minimum of $1,000) Dad insisted that I find a partner to invest with to take advantage of this high rate. My grandmother was delighted to add her small account to mine and now we both earn high interest. Also she does not pay taxes on the interest since the account is in my name.

We live next to a golf course and Dad is always finding golf balls in our garden. A few years ago he put me in charge of marketing the balls—I sell them to the neighbors and we split the proceeds 50/50. Now we grade the balls and package the best ones which we can sell at a higher price.

When we started doing this, we invested the proceeds in silver so I own several bars of silver. Now I add my share to the savings account to earn the higher interest.

My savings has grown so much that Dad has offered me a share of a single family rental home he is buying. He explained it all to me and I agreed to make my first real estate investment. I don't like the idea of vacancy or a repair so I hope my dad has selected a good manager.

I caddied in a golf tournament and made more money, and this summer I hope to get a contract to sell more golf balls and to work as a stock boy in my uncle's clothing store. By the time I go back to school I will have enough to buy some computer stocks.

I should mention that I get a $3-a-week allowance but none of this goes to my investments. I also have a large stamp collection and a number of $2 bills, both of which I hope will be valuable some day.

I like this business of making money and my dad has me keep records of all the transactions as well as prepare an annual forecast. It is fun learning about the business of investing and I'll never have to look back and say, "If only I'd started sooner!"

I believe in what Dad says, and if I can have a savings account, stocks, silver, real estate, stamps, currency and my own small business, you can too!

APPENDIX

The following is a list of additional sources of information which a good steward can use to keep up-to-date in the rapidly changing field of personal money management.

The Wall Street Journal

Success—The Magazine for Achievers
Box 2440, Boulder, CO 80321
Published monthly, about $14 per year.

Think & Grow Rich by Napoleon Hill

Audio cassette educational tapes
Learning is spaced repetition, and cassette tapes are time-efficient and productive. Many titles are published by SMI International Inc., Box 7614, Waco TX 76714

Local college or university extension programs
Call them and get on their mailing list of courses. *Everyone* should attend a basic income tax course—including income tax preparation—plus a minimum of *twenty hours* each year of formal continuing education on a subject of personal growth and development.

Financial or investment newsletters
None are specifically recommended. Many can be obtained free, others are available by subscription. Most people will read one for a year or so, then switch to another, as their knowledge changes. Newsletters do provide a good up-to-date source of concentrated information on a subject.

For those interested in entering the profession of financial counselling, further particulars can be obtained from

The International Association of Financial Planners
5775 Peachtree Dunwoody Rd. 120-C
Atlanta, GA 30342

The Society of Financial Consultants
P. O. Box 22842
Carmel, CA 93922